W9-ABN-021

Thinking Faith

Steps on the Way to a Philosophical Theology

FRITZ BURI

Translated by

Harold H. Oliver

FORTRESS PRESS   PHILADELPHIA

Translated from the German *Denkender Glaube*
by Fritz Buri, Verlag Paul Haupt, Bern, 1967.

© 1968 by Fortress Press, Philadelphia

Library of Congress Catalog Card Number 68-10984

5702H67   Printed in U.S.A.   1-990

Thinking Faith

Foreword

This volume is not the first summary and popularization of my theology. Two prior attempts at this have already appeared in English: *Theology of Existence,* trans. Harold H. Oliver and Gerhard Onder (Greenwood, South Carolina: Attic Press, 1965; German edition, 1954) and *Christian Faith in Our Time,* trans. Edward A. Kent (New York: Macmillan, 1966; German edition, 1952). The occasions which ultimately brought these projects, as well as my catechism, *Unterricht im Christlichen Glauben* (Bern: Verlag Paul Haupt, 1957), to print were primarily public lectures. *Christian Faith in Our Time* was given to the Basel public in 1950, and *Theology of Existence* to audiences in Copenhagen, Amsterdam, and Leiden in 1953. The present work comprises public lectures delivered at Drew University, Madison, New Jersey, where I was guest professor during the academic year, 1966-67. The material was published in German in early 1967 by the Verlag Paul Haupt, Bern.

From my perspective, all of these publications represent stations on the course of my theological thinking. Thus, they do not essentially differ from each other. The difference between *Theology of Existence* and *Thinking Faith* is more negligible than that between *Christian Faith in Our Time* and *Theology of Existence.* Though I studied with Rudolf Bultmann in 1928 and was quite early enamored of Karl Jaspers' philosophy, the influence of Albert Schweitzer and Martin Werner still dominates *Christian Faith in Our Time.* With the appearance of *Theology of Existence,* my decisive involvement with existential philosophy became apparent. This existential foundation has been further developed in *Thinking Faith.* Thus it is evident that the present approach through "believing existence" has resulted in a radical modification of the basic structure of my thinking.

The reader may find it helpful if I indicate these structural changes, since the proper outgrowth of this approach becomes evident only in the systematic sketch in the last chapter, placed there on account of the perspectives and problems considered in this volume. The priority of Christology in my present position is the main point of difference from the earlier volumes, though even now Christology remains indissolubly bound up with anthropology. Christology precedes the doctrines of God and of creation. In *Theology of Existence*—not to speak of *Christian Faith in Our Time*—this is not yet the case. In these two earlier proposals the classical schema is still preserved. In my Dogmatics (*Dogmatik als Selbstverständnis des Christlichen Glaubens,* Vol. I: *Vernunft und Offenbarung* [Bern: Verlag Paul Haupt, 1956]; Vol. II: *Der Mensch und die Gnade* [Bern: Verlag Paul Haupt, 1962]) this classical arrangement is rejected in favor of beginning the development of the positive system with the treatment of the redemption of man through Christ. The catechism exhibits this modification in its sequence of main headings: (1) knowledge, faith, and revelation; (2) man and sin; (3) reconciliation through Christ; (4) God and his creation; (5) the church and the kingdom of God.

This dogmatic system can be seen in the final chapter of the present volume, in which the presentation of Christian faith as a thinking faith makes it necessary for the title "Creation in Christ" to follow directly upon the initial treatment of the "Man of Faith." The reader will have to decide for himself what significance this particular christological orientation has for an understanding of the Christian faith as a thinking faith. This is no mere formal undertaking, but rather a thrust forward which involves great material consequences.

It is not necessary to stress this to American readers in view of the role being played in contemporary American theology by the existential-ontological ventures of John Macquarrie and the appeal to metaphysics through process philosophy by scholars such as Schubert Ogden, John B. Cobb, Jr., and Daniel Day Williams. As fascinating as these conceptions are, I am nevertheless not ready to adopt them. If I adopt, as I do, a christological ontology as the expression of the self-understanding of the Christian faith, I do not expose myself to the attacks of positivists and theothanitists. Ontologies and metaphysical systems which wish to be something other than ciphers for existence are able to withstand conceptual and linguistic analytical criticism only with great effort. The theothanitists can and may slay idols—but they probably do not wish to extinguish their own thinking self. They could and should become conscious of its finitude and so attain to a "theology after the death of the absolute ego."

It should be evident from a comparison of this volume with another of my works appearing simultaneously from Fortress Press, *How Can We Still Speak Responsibly of God?* that I am presently at a station on the course of my theological thinking which I hope will not be the last. In the chapter of the other volume entitled "The Reality of Faith"—originally a lecture given at the Harvard Divinity School—I develop insights concerning the problem of objectifying and objectivity which became clearer to me in conversations at Yale University with my former Basel student, Charley Hardwick. These insights have not yet attained comparable clarity in this present volume, but are nevertheless approached here with an appropriate understanding of their epistemological elements.

In living thought one must always remain open to surprises and modifications. Such a course is undertaken as a risk—but also with the joy of discovery! We are not at the end, but on the way. What I expect are not heralds of my thought, nor unsympathetic critics, but rather companions who critically think with me.

It was not always easy for me to go the way on which my thought and faith led—although not because of its inherent difficulties, for these worked more as impulses to further progress. Problems are sources of power or, in modern technological jargon, they work as the motor of thought. "If my last doubt should die, so would my faith also die"—these words from the progressive thought of Gottfried Keller have made a deep impression on me (cf. my *Gottfried Kellers Glaube* [Bern: Verlag Paul Haupt, 1944]). And, similarly, the words of Carl Spitteler are to be remembered: "Well-motivated is he, who is deep and alert" and "My heart says, 'Nevertheless!'" (cf. my *Prometheus und Christus* [Bern: Verlag A. Francke, 1945]).

In those years when I found comfort in poets, Europe had its political dictators and concentration camps. But we survived. Though initially distant both geographically and theologically from Karl Barth, in Basel I came spiritually closer to him. I lectured in the same university where he taught his *Dogmatik* chapter by chapter, while American students flocked to Basel. I preached from the same pulpit of the Cathedral from which Eduard Thurneysen preached with great popularity. We were colleagues in the university and in the community, fought many hard battles, and over a glass of wine smoked many pipefuls of tobacco together in friendship. We learned to take notice of each other—if each in his own way. And so the years passed, and in their course much of a different sort has happened—in the world and in the church.

In the summer of 1963, I had a surprise visit from Dean Stanley Hopper of Drew University, in consequence of which I was invited to participate in the 1964 Drew Consultation on "The Problem of Non-Objectifying Thinking and Speaking in Contemporary Theology." Heinrich Ott, Barth's successor at Basel, also attended the same conference as representative of a theology which appeals to Heidegger's "non-objectifying speaking." I contested this possibility from the perspective of Jaspers' philosophy, affirming in so doing the "objectivity" of all our speaking. Although we came from the same place, Ott and I stood over against each other at Drew as representatives of two quite different hermeneutical theories which still understand each other and are bound up together in more than a purely theoretical way. We were both later invited to be guest professors at the Graduate School of Drew University.

The seven months which, in 1966 and 1967, my wife and I spent on the campus of Drew University belong to the happiest of our lives, both personally and professionally. We were free from pastoral and other duties and could live for study and ourselves, and for all that is interesting, endearing, amazing, and even frightening in many regions of the American continent. I was delighted with the openness and keenness of the students, and we enjoyed the kindness and gracious hospitality of colleagues and their families. Not even certain administrative difficulties which struck Drew University at that time were able to disturb this impression and this good will. I feel compelled here to express deep gratitude to the administration, colleagues, and assistants at Drew for everything which they offered us. It was more than what we offered them, and we shall be attached to that place for life. And even though the equestrian statue of Francis Asbury, which I frequently passed in the early morning hours, was occasionally bedecked with crepe, the pioneer spirit which is captured on the inscription of this memorial still lives at Drew—and not only at Drew, but also at the many other schools and seminaries which we visited in America.

It was our impression that American theologians are not only like the Athenians of Paul's day who were constantly interested in "hearing and saying what is quite new," but they are genuinely *open* to what is new. Knowledge must be verified by experiment, and for the spirit who dares to make the test, there lies behind every horizon a new one yet to be explored. For this reason the so-called Neo-Orthodox theology represents a closed experiment for Americans. Theology which counts today moves in other directions—even if it has derived and will continue to derive rich benefit out of that movement. Whether what goes by the name of "New Frontier Theology" really lives up to the name is another question. Nevertheless, to me there appear to be very promising courses for the "new theology."

For several years American theology has set out for new

shores. It has weighed anchor and is on course. It is a joy for me to be acquainted personally with the different voyagers. Where does the course lead? This must be asked, and in view of the many diverse elements in American theology, one has every reason to pose the question. Phenomena are met here which call for serious thought—not only because they are risky but because they wish to be considered.

This is the way I felt concerning *Thinking Faith,* which was in manuscript form before my departure for America, even before my acquaintance with the theology of the American continent. In America I associated with men who are aware of the same problems and who pose the same questions. And even though they may use different methods and reach different answers, they have not "arrived," but are ready to risk a mental experiment which is simultaneously an experiment in life. To the modern European, America today seems no longer so much the land of unlimited possibilities as the land of unlimited problems. In its expanse of dawning horizons and the overwhelming magnitude of its many dimensions—in daily life as well as in the high points of a discussion, in the world of technology and politics as well as in the world of the spirit— one can feel dizzy or lost. But *cogito ergo sum*—not in abstract thought, but in a thinking in concrete reality, a thinking which proves its worth in daily praxis. Here existence occurs which, to the extent that this thinking presses to the extremities, and recognizes its appointed limits, becomes believing thinking. It is, however, not merely a believing thinking, but a thinking of the Christian faith, though it dares to put that tradition in this framework and attempts so to understand it. Where this occurs we remain not single individuals, but members of a community—a living community with the past and a community with those present for a new future. Thus we can "sing the Lord's song" even "in a strange land."

Now I am back again at home within my own four walls. The thoughts which I have written here ran through my mind last evening during a Mozart serenade in the cloister of the Cathedral. Under the Gothic arches in the twilight, my eyes

scanned the cenotaph bedecked walls and stopped quite unconsciously at that of the great systematician of Reformed
Orthodoxy, Polanus of Polansdorf, whose name is familiar
to readers of Barth's *Dogmatik*. "What has become of the
heritage of the Fathers today?" I had to ask myself. I was
conscious that nearby was buried Sebastian Castellio who fled
Calvin's Geneva to Basel. Quite near is also the cenotaph of
the Antistes, Jacob Burckhardt, the father of the Jacob Burckhardt who wrote *Weltgeschichtlichen Betrachtungen* (Medita-
tions on World History) and *Renaissance in Italien*. Down
below, the Rhine flowed past the Cathedral as it always does,
the river upon which I look now on this radiant summer morning from the tall window of the study of the manse over whose
door stands the date, 1531.

These are the walls within which *Thinking Faith* emerged,
and these are the spirits who saw it come into being. I think it
has not been superfluous to give the reader of this volume a
look at the environs of its origin, and to let him hear the
rustling and the music of the stream of history which is today
neither dead nor silent, but a living, warning present. Though
he may find this heritage quite unromantic, the American
reader may find much in my thought that is understandable—
and hopefully not to his detriment.

In front of my window the Rhine flows on until it empties
eventually into the ocean, on the other side of which I see in
my mind's eye the Statue of Liberty. That statue does not turn
away from America, as it was explained to me last winter by a
citizen of that country, but rather just as it was originally
intended it stands as an earnest of the freedom of a new
Promised Land. Such an experience of freedom was my visit to
America, especially in the spiritual community which I experienced at Drew University, where I delivered the material
of this volume as public lectures. There there seems to me to be
soil in which this plant can take root, grow, and bear fruit. This
little book is therefore dedicated to all my friends in America
as a token of my deep appreciation and genuine affection.

Basel   Fritz Buri
Summer, 1967

Table of Contents

1

Thinking as Knowing

What is thinking? When we ask this question, we already enact that about which the sentence asks. We wish to know what thinking is—and thereby we think, for there is no knowledge without thought. When we inquire about thinking, we are already in the midst of thought. But one can disregard this circular situation and speak about thinking from quite different perspectives.

DIFFERENT CONCEPTS OF THINKING

Thinking can be investigated physiologically; that is, according to its physical, corporeal nature. Thinking is an operation which takes place in specific parts of the brain. Our question is then a concern of neurology. It is certainly valid to seek the nature of thinking in this way, for thinking is naturally connected with the body. We are made aware of this when, having a headache or because of the weather, we say, "I cannot think today." In our thinking we are surely determined by our physical condition and thus by specific states and operations in our body. One does not always feel like thinking.

This suggests that something else apparently intervenes between the body and thinking, namely, just that which makes one feel like thinking or not, i.e., one's mood. Mood is something psychic. Thinking can thus be investi-

1

gated psychologically, that is, in respect to its connection with the psyche. There is a psychology of thinking in which one speaks of emotive thinking, a thinking which is determined by certain emotional states. We know of this from experience. We also know about a thinking that is related to the operations investigated by depth psychology. We can stand, in our thinking, under specific compulsions, pre-molded forms for our thinking. Since time immemorial, perhaps even without being aware of it, men have been stamped in their thinking by so-called archetypes.

Here we have indicated yet another way in which thinking can be conceived. This investigation of the forms of thought by depth psychology was not always known, and our thinking has also certainly been molded by its discoveries. There is, however, a history of thought extending from ancient times, through all historically conceivable epochs to the present, and our present thinking itself will develop further. This history of thinking is biographically evident in the development of thinking in our own lives. The Apostle Paul was aware of this when he wrote, "When I was a child, I thought like a child and had child-like aims. But when I became a man, I put away what was childish" (1 Cor. 13:11). Furthermore, the history of thinking can also be documented in the development of entire epochs. Modern man thinks differently from primitive or medieval man. Cultural history shows us the different thought-forms which have emerged and then have had to make way for other forms.

Thinking can also be conceived sociologically, that is, in connection with the forms of society, with the forms of the material and spiritual presuppositions of the society. Man in the East thinks differently from man in the West. Man thinks differently in different situations. There are indeed sociological presuppositions for thinking.

But all of the possibilities envisaged in the sequence—physiological, psychological, historical, sociological aspects of thinking—all of these presuppose and utilize thinking.

There are, to be sure, two extreme boundaries for thinking.

Certain of the methods for conceiving of thinking which have been mentioned can be mechanically enacted with the aid of specifically constructed apparatus. The most modern contrivance in this regard is the computer, a kind of thinking machine which yields results no man can produce. But even in the construction and use of such miracle machines, man participates with his thinking.

The same is true also of the other limit, which we may set over against the computer, namely, that thinking which asserts of itself that it is not merely human thinking, but the thinking of the World-Mind (or Spirit) which unfolds itself through the finite mind in order to come to itself by taking up this self-estrangement. Today such a conception of thinking is met in a different, but corresponding, form when it is said, "Language thinks, language speaks, in language Being occurs, Being speaks in thinking." But even this philosophy of Being and of language-event employs thinking.

In respect to the difficulties which emerge here we may call on Goethe's maxim:

> How do you fare so well in the world?
> You say: so well you have done it all;
> My child, I have done very well in the world,
> For I have not thought about thinking at all![1]

But even when one wishes in this way to dispense with thinking, satirizing all the efforts of the self-reflection of thinking, he must use thinking to do so.

We cannot escape the fact that when we talk about

---

[1] *Goethes Werke*, Sophien Ausgabe, Vol. 5, Part 1, Aus dem Nachlass, Zahme Xenien, page 92.

thinking we are already engaged in thought. If we wish to clarify the nature of thinking, we can do so only by asking what thinking is in its enactment.

THINKING IN ITS ENACTMENT

How is it with thinking that we already enact it when we pose this question? This thinking does not simply happen, like the rain outside, for example. "It" does not think as "it rains"—even though there may be a kind of unconscious thinking as, for example, when in sleep we continue to think about something: we fall asleep with a problem and in the morning the solution has been found. The brain apparently continues to work. There is a kind of dreamlike thinking about which the depth psychologists know.

We can speak of thinking in a genuine sense, however, only when we responsibly participate in it, when *we* enact it. To be sure, we can also think dependently—as under compulsion. Although there are bridges between them, there is nevertheless a difference between an alien thought which draws me into its course, develops within me, and is expressed through me, and a thought by which I am moved but over against which I stand at a certain distance, conscious of the fact that I am thinking rather than that it is thinking in me. I am the subject of my thinking. I am extremely bound up with what is thought and with what somehow thinks in me, but there is still this "I" which enacts the thinking, and this thinking does not occur unless I am there. We can let our thoughts take their own course, not "be there," not "think along with them"—but it is we who are "not there," who are "not thinking along with them." It is not *something* that has dreamed, but rather *I* who have dreamed. We can lose ourselves in thought—but it is we in any case who awake and find our-

4

selves again. We can be enthralled with something or bored, but it is we who accomplish this act.

Just as it is certain that it is I who think, so it is certain that I always think *something*. Thinking always has an object. The subject which thinks has an object toward which it directs itself. Even if this object should prove to be a phantom, it is *something* nevertheless, an object over against me. And it is equally certain that this object hangs together with this subject and is determined by it. These connections of subject and object pose very complicated questions for the theory of cognition. For example, to what extent is objective thinking, or objective conceptualizing of reality, possible, and to what extent is such thinking already formed by our ideas and concepts? However that may be, thinking always occurs in this polarity of subject and object. At the moment we *think* a *thought*, we are already in this scheme. We can even speak about this subject-object scheme, and thus conceive it as an object. But while we enact this thinking about the subject-object scheme we are already thinking in this scheme. It is always present with our thinking.

When I begin to think, I think something; and as long as I think, I do not escape this I-object relationship. I am never the absolute "I" but also never a mere object, never only a computer, and never Being itself, *the* Mind (Spirit). We become aware of this when we make mistakes—something a computer never does!—and when we become aware of the finiteness of our mind, about which we probably cannot deceive ourselves.

In this way we have already taken a second step in the development of our thought. We began with the different possibilities of speaking about thinking—physiological, psychological, historical, and sociological—and we have discovered that, even in the extremities represented by the computer and the event of Being, discourse about thinking always presupposes thinking and is enacted within it. And we have also established that the enactment of this thinking always occurs in the realm of subject and object; that is, when I think, I think *something*. But even though I and the object are inextricably connected to each other, so we never exchange places with the object of our thinking, not even when we think about ourselves. But it is by now already clear to us that we are constantly something different from what we think ourselves to be, and that we cannot exchange places with the object nor the object with us.

In both of the steps we have now taken, we have placed at our disposal certain specific aids which obviously belong to thinking, and therewith we come to the third step in our discussion of the nature of thinking, viz., in thinking we make use of concepts.

THE CONCEPTUALITY OF THINKING

The attempt can be made—even at the extremities—to think without concepts, as we have employed them here in the sense of designations of specific contents. Without such concepts and merely on the basis of vague ideas we can ask what thinking is. Even in this situation one thereby naturally represents something to himself, for otherwise he would not be preoccupied with the question at all. One has distinct expectations and questions; one represents something to himself of which he has read and with which he is occupied. It is the case that with everything of which we attempt to think in clear, univocal concepts we first have an impression, a representation, an image of it.

There are powerful images in which whole ages have thought. There were times in which the myths, the divine sagas, were still vital. It can be asked whether religion or faith is possible at all without these worlds of images, whether myth is not the legitimate language of faith. We shall have opportunity to return to this question later. Here we need to consider the following statement: We have certain perceptions of the outer and inner world, of a sensible or mental sort, in specific representations. We know something; something is known by us, given to us—partially produced by us in our experience and thinking, partially taken in from outside. At the moment we shall disregard the complicated question of how the inner and outer are related to each other, and only establish that in concepts we attempt to conceive distinct traits of an object, so that we have not only fleeting impressions and representations, but univocal designations. With the help of such designations we are in a position to construct the contents of perceptions and objects of awareness not only for ourselves but also for others, so that we can agree on what we mean. For example: we designate a certain space a "lecture hall," or the word "auditorium" can be used. But the same space cannot be called a "church" or a "cafe." Everyone knows that the terms "cafe," "church," and "lecture hall" mean different things and cannot be interchanged.

Such designations have grown up over the years. We have taken them over with the language, and language is something living and developing. But it does not simply toy with things and change arbitrarily, as fantasy likes to do. Language is given to us not only for poetry and fantasy but also for understanding things which we wish to know precisely and without confusion. For this purpose concepts are used, whether they arise by means of abstraction from the content of consciousness, or whether they are already pre-formed in us. There are different theories about their origin. But in any case concepts facilitate the use of language; this is not all they do, but this is highly significant for us. Language transmits terms to us by which we can designate specific items univocally, and by their aid we can relocate something in something else, with the result that we are thus able to know. To return to our example: I do not seek merely a lecture hall of which I have a vague impression; rather, with the aid of its number I find the specific lecture hall which I seek. And even when the concern is not with a lecture hall for mathematics but with one for philosophy or theology, that which is heard in it hopefully moves not merely in vague impressions, but employs clear, univocal conceptuality so that one can know what is going on.

The concept puts us in a position to rediscover one thing in another, and to know it univocally as that which it is. This is accomplished by supplying the concept with a designation which has been agreed upon in a system of signs. The nature of the concept consists in the univocal designation made possible by it for the intended object. The operation by which one comes to such a univocal designation by means of concepts is called "judgment." In order to arrive at valid judgments, concepts are brought into relation to each other. By testing the relation of these concepts to reality, one seeks to emerge from a world of mere fantasy. Although the concept and the judgments are quite different from the reality they designate, they nevertheless help us to orient ourselves with respect to this reality. We are able not only to communicate the results to each other, but also to test the reality together.

THE FOUR GROUND RULES OF LOGIC

For this use of the concept there are distinct laws which thinking does not invent, but which rather belong to its nature and which it cannot evade if it wishes to remain thought. Thus it belongs to the nature of the concept that within a judgmental situation it must become immutably established that, for example, I cannot suddenly equate the numerical value of three with nine. One can certainly give a different meaning to a specific item, but within a specific judgmental situation I have to retain the previously established significance if the concept is to fulfill its function as a univocal designation. That is the logical principle of identity. It affirms that within a fixed judgmental operation a fixed referent must be maintained and not arbitrarily changed.

Another principle of thinking is the law of the forbidden contradiction, which says that two contradictory judgments cannot both be true at the same time. One or the other is false. *Tertium non datur.*

The same is dealt with in the principle of the excluded middle: Two judgments, one of which affirms what the other denies, cannot both be true.

Furthermore, there belongs here the principle of sufficient reason which states that from a specific premise a specific conclusion will follow, and that if the premise changes so also will the conclusion. An effect has its cause, a cause has its effects, and if one is lacking, the other is lacking also.

These are the four so-called ground rules of logic: the principle of identity, of the forbidden contradiction, of the excluded middle, and of sufficient reason. Even those who question these basic rules of logic—and that goes on continually—make use of these laws. They are always present in the enactment of thinking, and they belong unconditionally to the nature of the thinking about which we have come to some agreement. Whoever wishes to prove that the principle of identity is not valid cannot abandon that which is so designated and suddenly represent to himself something different from what was first assumed. Whoever says that logic is contradictory, or that there are things which are not logically conceivable, uses logic to do so. There are, of course, things which cannot be conceived logically. However, even for these pronouncements, recourse is had to these ground rules of logic. The act of questioning the basic principles of logic presupposes their validity and thereby contradicts itself.

THE DEMAND OF METHODICAL APPROPRIATENESS

But now, even as it is necessary to take into account these rules of logic, we must also give constant consideration to the peculiar characteristics of each object of thinking. We may not use the same methods and the same concepts in speaking about all things. Whoever attempts to do so will discover that concepts which are very illuminating in one instance say nothing to us in another, or that methods which are highly productive in one instance prove to be completely useless in another. The same methods are not appropriate for the chemistry laboratory and for the analysis of a poem. A poem can be fed into a computer, but it is likely that no deep understanding of the poem will result. Furthermore, one is not able to write poetry with a computer.

It is the nature of thinking that it has to adapt its concepts and its methods to its objects. In every instance we have to give attention to the important distinction between what is quantitatively measurable in natural science and what is qualitatively experienced in, for example, history, history presenting precisely an object in which both methods certainly have a place. To history belongs the enumeration of years and other measurable things, but in these the nature of history is not grasped. History cannot be learned and evaluated at a distance; rather, genuine historical understanding presupposes actual participation in history. Here are two quite different concepts of history: the historical facts, and the history in which man is himself a participant.

But it is precisely this historical investigation which shows us that—even with the most adequately formulated methods—we are never able conclusively to conceive the object. Certainly there are some results of which it can be said, "This is a fact; that happened at such and such a time." But how it occurred and in what connection—about these things there are always new conceptions. A specific historical event which is established in its date and external course may be quite variously interpreted. The victor makes history. All is interpretation, all explanation. In any case, the humanities must be conscious of the subjective factors in and, accordingly, of the relativity of their knowledge.

The same holds true for the quantitative factors of the natural sciences. Naturally the morality of the investigator in a laboratory—if he sticks pretty much to the business at hand—has no influence upon the operations which take place in his retorts; but the same cannot be said for the investigator of a specific item of cultural history. The humanities, like the natural sciences, because of the inextinguishable subjectivity of the investigator and the non-finality of the research, must be constantly conscious of their non-finality. Otherwise they would cease to be sciences and become superstitions.

In this way we have now come to a further step. The logical-conceptual thinking which has been developed from the nature of thought and which employs both the basic laws of thinking and the methods which correspond to its object—this thinking also has its boundaries, both relative and absolute.

THE RELATIVE AND ABSOLUTE BOUNDARIES OF SCIENTIFIC THINKING

Relativity is the fourth characteristic of conceptual thinking. Methodical scientific thinking is never finished because it never completely comprehends its object and because it is always somehow conditioned by the subject. The boundaries can certainly be continually pushed back;

knowledge can always increase. Not only do new possibilities constantly emerge in the sphere of investigation but the object also manifests itself from quite different angles.

The exact sciences presuppose a specific system of coordinates by which they register their results. This system of coordinates is, however, never absolute, and even the most exact results are valid only under definite presuppositions. If the conditions of a series of experiments are altered, or if new realities are disclosed through technical possibilities, then the prior presuppositions are jeopardized. Physics, for example, today requires completely new reconstructions of its picture of the world, and if it wishes to remain a science it must not seal up these constructions in a so-called scientific world-view but hold them open.

These limits are relative. Great agreement about them is possible. Research can become exact and can be extended. But at two points cognitive thinking, as we have described it, presses to its primordial limits which cannot be transcended, limits characterized by the two poles within which it is enacted, namely, self and Being.

The subject, the thinking "I," can ultimately never be made the object of thinking. Man is always just as he understands himself. He is not primordially determined in his nature. Scientifically, man can be said to be determined in certain aspects: physiologically, psychologically, culturally, sociologically, etc. But he always has the possibility of understanding himself in each specific way and thereby of becoming what he is.

The other point at which thinking reaches an absolute limit, and of which it must remain conscious if it wishes to remain thinking, is the totality of Being, the totality of the object-world. We always see only a section of it from a specific point of view. Even what has been unfolded here has been received and understood by each reader in terms of his own presuppositions. But the totality of Being, the totality of the spiritual world, the totality of reality, the entirety of nature, is unattainable as an object.

The two poles of the subject-object scheme, within which all thinking which deserves the name occurs, are not comprehensible for this thinking. The "I" and the totality of Being form its unconditional, absolute boundaries.

THE SEQUENCE OF THEMES

From these findings there results the series of themes which we wish to develop in the following. We have now spoken about thinking, its nature and limits. Its absolute, fixed limits are the "I" and Being, man and the world-as-a-whole. In its treatment of man and the world, a thinking which knows its limits is aware that it is dealing with something which is not merely its object. Whenever we speak of man and the world we have to do with that which transcends all that can be objectively and conceptually grasped. This beyond to which man and the world point is designated in the language of mythology and religion as God. We call thinking which transcends *faith*. A faith which enacts this transcending in thinking is a thinking faith. Man, world, and God are the themes of this faith.

We are engaged in a quest for ourselves, the world, and God because we know that we can otherwise miss the meaning of our existence (*Dasein*). It is the primordial intention of faith to discover the meaning of our existence and to enable us to act in such a way as not to miss this meaning. In this respect the question of good and evil arises. That is good which enables me to actualize the meaning of my existence; everything which destroys it is evil. Therefore the question of good and evil is a question of faith. It is closely connected with the further question of why there is evil at all, that is, why there is the possibility of the destruction of meaning, of the loss of meaning. When the question is related to God it is the quest for

13

theodicy, for the justification of God. As shocking as it may seem, theologians and philosophers have attempted from time to time to justify God. It is the quest for the meaning of history toward which we continually press and which stirs every thinking person.

These are all simultaneously and perennially the questions of the Christian faith. That faith deals with man as the image of God and with the world as God's creation. It deals not only with God the Creator, but also with God the Redeemer. Christian faith is therefore concerned with sin and reconciliation, and with the kingdom of God. It is not without good reason that the Fourth Gospel uses the designation Logos, the Word, for Christ. We deal with this Logos when, as in the foregoing, we speak about *logic,* and it will accompany us along the entire way which we have now begun to tread.[2]

---

[2] Relevant to this treatment are two small volumes by Karl Jaspers: *Way to Wisdom,* trans. Ralph Manheim (New Haven: Yale University Press, 1951), which is comprised of radio addresses delivered in Basel in 1950, and a series of lectures for German television published in 1965 under the title, *Kleine Schule des philosophischen Denkens.* To be mentioned is also my own *Theology of Existence* (cf. above p. v.). Martin Heidegger's *Was heisst Denken?* (Tübingen, 1954) should be contrasted with the view developed here.

2

Man — A Boundary of Knowledge

What is man? This theme emerges for us out of the discussion of the nature of knowledge and its boundaries. We have seen that cognition, or knowing, which is enacted in concepts and judgments and is directed toward its content in its methods and categories, presses necessarily toward boundaries. There are, first, boundaries of a relative kind which can be extended and which advance like the horizon for a traveler, always, however, in such a way that this horizon of knowing extends itself, so that knowing can never circumvent its own horizon and never occupy an absolute, final position. It is by the recognition of these relative, shifting boundaries that the absoluteness of the boundaries of our knowing becomes evident. This happens in a sphere which is determined by the standpoint of the knower and by the horizon which circumscribes the open realm of what is to be known. It occurs constantly in a scheme in which subject and object are related, although both this cogitating subject and the totality of being resist objectification.

Now we may ask, "What is this subject engaged in knowing, this subject which is something more than simply the place at which knowing is enacted?" It consists not only of understanding and reason and that which through understanding and reason is known objectively. In thinking faith there is a transcending to still quite different spheres of reality.

THE SIGNIFICANCE OF THE ANTHROPOLOGICAL APPROACH

If we begin to unfold the nature of thinking faith by asking the question "What is man?" we are nevertheless aware that another starting point could be selected, namely, that other absolute boundary of our knowledge, Being-in-its-totality. We should justify our choice of a point of departure, for it is not self-evident that we should begin with man, the subjective pole, rather than with the objective pole, Being-in-its-totality. Why this priority of man?

It is always man who makes pronouncements about Being and who is so much a part of Being that he is the existent who knows about Being. We do not know whether other existents know of their involvement in Being. However that may be, we are of the opinion that, so far as we can tell, only man has to do with Being in such a way as to know of his own Being. It is certainly of far-reaching significance for the whole character of thinking, and especially for a faith closely connected with this thinking, that it gives precedence to man rather than to Being. This decision is of significance for the totality of this thinking.

When we inquire about the nature of thinking with man as our starting point, we are repeating what has transpired at the crucial junctures of the history of philosophy. It was already a feature of Greek philosophy that the one who thought about Being was replaced by the thinker who turned his attention toward man. The first Greek philosophers sought the rational principle of Being after being freed from the myths which spoke of the primordial origin of Being. It was only when a Socrates emerged that attention was especially turned toward the question of man.

Something similar occurred with the rise of modern philosophy: a philosophy of consciousness replaced the medieval thinking about Being. A similar contrast presented
itself in our time when the systems of world-views were
replaced by a thinking that focused its special attention on
the existence of man. When we begin with the question of
the nature of man we stand in the line of the anthropological thinking of the Sophists as opposed to that of the pre-
Socratics, of the modern era's thinking of consciousness as
opposed to that of medieval Scholasticism, and of the contemporary thinking about existence which emerged with
the disintegration of traditional world-views.

If this question is posed in a methodical, scientific way,
then we are dealing with anthropology, that is, with the
science of man. But anthropology can be practiced under
very different aspects and with correspondingly different
methods, much as is the case with respect to cognition as
we have developed it. In this science two quite different
kinds of anthropology stand opposed: one modeled after
the natural sciences and the other after the humanities;
and within these two major areas still further subdivisions
and specializations appear. But despite the multitude of
the anthropological systems and the special interest which
is focused today on this special scientific-philosophical
area, we become conscious of the problematical character of
this undertaking when we consider that man—like
Being-in-its-totality—is just that kind of being which ultimately cannot be objectified. But how is a science of something nonobjectifiable possible? Actually, the problem of
all anthropology consists in the fact that here the knowledge appropriate to objective matters of science turns its
attention to an object which as such is something different
from, that is, more than, an object. Or put pictorially:
How can the eye, which sees everything, see itself? It is the
difficult task of anthropology to show with respect to this

problem how the nature of man can be appropriately discussed, and how the question "What is man?" can be answered.

The question about man is posed not only out of a scientific interest. When we ask "What is man?" we always somehow include ourselves, in which case we somehow have in view our own experience, our own problems, our own life situation. What are we actually? Why are we a riddle to ourselves? What is the meaning of our existence? We desire to obtain from anthropology not only some special explanations but ultimately an answer to these basic questions of our existence. Can science or even scientific anthropology furnish an answer to this question?

MAN IN MYTH

Before there was a scientific concern about man there were answers to these questions in the realm of myth—answers which seem fantastic to us today. All cultures and religions provide such prescientific, often picturesque stories which describe where man came from, how he emerged, and something of his destiny.

Myths are to be distinguished from science by the fact that they are unaware of precisely that subject-object scheme which belongs to the nature of scientific thinking. What to us—scientifically seen—appears as an object appeared there as a subject. The world seemed personified. The forces and powers of the occurrence emerged as demons, spirits, and gods, and men were viewed as objects of these supernatural subjects. We are aware of the demythologizing of this world-view which took place in its own development, a development characterized by the transformation of what was previously subject—namely gods, demons, angels, spirits—into objects; and conversely, of what was previously an object of this supernatural world, into the subject of our knowing. At a specific age the child frees himself from the personification of his environment in order to speak as an "I." This awareness of the subjective-objective world-structure of our consciousness emerges in our biographical development at that time when the world is no longer animated by some kind of supernatural force or power, and we learn to say "I." In the realm of myth the world is a totality, and in the sphere of this unified world the myth explains how men were formed by the gods, with what destinies they were endowed, and from whence come the riddles of existence.

Out of the inexhaustible treasury of the myths of all times and peoples we select the following example: The Incas tell that the gods created man in three attempts. First, out of clay. But these were dumb. So they broke up these first men as a child breaks up his clay models. Then they made a second attempt and carved man out of wood. But these became coarse and wicked so the gods had to destroy man again. But some escaped the destruction and fled to the forests and there became apes. Then the gods made a third attempt to create man and for this he used dough. This dough produced clever and crafty men, and although the gods could not be perfectly satisfied with them, they were tired of creating and so let them live. But they clouded the brains of these men and therefore— despite their cleverness—mistakes and errors are possible for them.

Other myths explain the special origin and fate of man in other ways. All, however, seek to explain what is special about man, i.e., that he manipulates, knows of evil, knows modesty, can laugh and cry, knows of his death, possesses speech, makes tools, gives rise to culture, and other such *anthropina*.

The Greeks explain how man, through Prometheus, gained possession of fire and hence of technology, how thereby the jealousy of the gods was aroused, and how Prometheus—the bringer of salvation—was impaled on the Caucusus by the gods who as punishment allowed an eagle to tear at his ever-renewed liver.

This image of the suffering bearer of salvation reminds us of the Christian mythology which has achieved such great significance for our Western culture. From the form-critical perspective it deals with a parallel product of poetic fantasy in which man tries to give an answer to the ultimate question of his nature. The biblical record also deals with the creation of man out of clay and depicts him as a being who aroused God's displeasure, was therefore excluded from Paradise, and was later punished by the flood. Even here a figure emerges who wishes to give man what he has been denied by God, namely, the knowledge of good and evil, so as to be like God. The serpent which promises such to man is envisaged, therefore, as something of a redeemer-figure.

There have been times in which it was thought possible to find in the story of Adam the datable beginning of the history of mankind; and there were great historical works, which dated world history from that event, conceived along these lines in the ancient and medieval church. Through the centuries, man's view of himself has certainly been stamped by this biblical story of the creation of man in Paradise and the loss of his original perfection as punishment for his disobedience, and we all still somehow grow up under the influence of this story.

SCIENTIFIC AND NATURALISTIC-MONISTIC ANTHROPOLOGY

But today we know how this biblical picture of man as being under the influence of powerful spiritual—and often not so spiritual—forces has been called into question by a natural science which has replaced it with one quite different. We have only to recall the name of Charles

Darwin who published his famous work, *On The Origin of Species*, around the middle of the last century, and his still more important work, *The Descent of Man*, in 1871. In the latter he established the thesis that not only did the different forms of life develop out of each other, but that man also belongs within this development and descended from a particular kind of ape. In this connection a whole library has developed, both scientific and unscientific in character. In the most famous work to arise in this field, *The Riddle of the Universe*, written by Ernst Häckel in 1899, anthropology forms part of zoology. Through this anthropology, carried out by the natural sciences in the last century, the traditional biblical-Christian view of man has become problematical.

Instead of depicting man springing suddenly as a finished product out of the hand of God, these theories of natural science show how man has developed progressively through millions of years to his present condition. Here no supernatural factors are needed to explain the degree of differentiation achieved by this special branch of organic life; rather, everything can be explained in natural ways which follow natural laws. The descent of man from the animal world is explained naturally by natural methods which take into account infinitely long spans of time within which the transitions disappear. The principle of this anthropology of the natural sciences can be comprehended in the formula, "Man is nothing other than. . . ."

When the various positions are compared, the essential characteristics of the individual epochs are reflected. The reaction of anti-idealism saw man as nothing other than matter; the subsequent age of the machine, nothing other than a machine; Marxism, only a creature economically determined by hunger; the age of imperialism, nothing other than "will to power"; that of Freud, only libido; that of anxiety, nothing other than anxiety.

21

This "nothing other than" is not only that which is most noticeable but that which gained for these positions a certain ingress and popularity. People sit up and take notice whenever a uniform, univocal explanation is offered for complex relationships and operations. It is characteristic of these scientific ways of explaining man that they all have a monistic-naturalistic character. Complex interrelationships are traced back to one principle, hence their monism; and this principle is explained by natural laws, hence their naturalism.

These anthropologies have specific ethical consequences. If man is nothing but an animal—perhaps a very developed, perhaps even depraved, animal—then such an insight can be received as a kind of release from moral obligations. Therefore, noblesse oblige is unimportant and we do not need to be anything other than what we are. Everything is natural, for everything can be explained and justified. If we are only creatures of nature then we should live according to nature and not be ashamed of this natural character of life. Even if this signifies a liberation in certain aspects, it is at the same time fraught with the danger of a leveling and abandoning of that which according to other formulations belongs to the nature of man. The ethical consequences of this naturalistic monism are such that man is probably freed from a certain "uneasiness about culture," but together with this uneasiness is released from culture altogether.

For this reason a certain resistance has arisen to such a naturalistic-monistic conception of man. Over against the primitively formulated "ape-theory" it has been simply asked whether that creature is still an ape who has learned that he is no longer an ape. The question points to a specific "missing link" in this so well-known and explainable chain of cause and effect development: How then are the transitions between the individual steps to be explained?

Are there not major differences?

In order to meet this objection, the naturalistic conception has developed an additional theory which designates the spirit that is critical of mere nature as a decadent product of the development, a disintegration of the good breeding of the animal. The understanding is not only regarded as a substitute for the absent instinct. As Ludwig Klages has expressed it, it is a mental "contradictor of the soul"; or as Nietzsche said, there is an "illness" in man. Prior to Nietzsche, Christian theologians had come to a similar evaluation when, for example, Augustine regarded man in original sin as a sick creature. For these thinkers the spirit presented no human advantage. As a spiritual being man is not the highest developed creature but a depraved, fallen being—or as Theodor Lessing said, "a species of robber ape which has become extremely insane."

Despite all the errors and excesses of this monistic naturalism, the notion of the development of man from lower forms of life is still generally accepted today. And even though no prudent scientist today would simply repeat Darwin or Häckel, no one is in a position to deny the doctrine of evolution as it was basically validated by these men.

IDEALISTIC-DUALISTIC ANTHROPOLOGY OF SPIRIT

Before we undertake a further development we wish briefly to examine the opposite of the naturalistic-monistic anthropology. This position was already alluded to when we spoke of a rejection of the naturalistic theory and of the critical questions which were raised against it, particularly those which asked whether man is not something different from nature. If he is also nature, a product of nature, a development, does nature know about this natural development? Must man be merely what he is according to the interrelationships conceivable by natural science? Is not the nature of man so constituted that he knows not only of his naturalness—by a knowledge which is not simply nature—but also that as a mind he has to be actualized over against nature and the life of his environment in order to become first what he is destined to be? This destiny to be fulfilled is something different from that which results from natural relationships. Man is realized in that which points beyond the earthly and natural to something beyond time—something eternal and divine, though always, to be sure, in earthly historical forms. Thus in this conception which opposes that of naturalistic monism, man always has a dualistic character, i.e., he is composed of nature and mind (*Geist*). The mental is something conceived as surpassing nature, as that which puts its stamp upon the natural at its disposal. Through the spiritual spark in man a supernatural, eternal, and divine factor is active in the world.

This view of man, which is to be termed idealistic because of its emphasis upon the spirit, or mind, has assumed various forms in the course of history. Naturalism, as described, was directed against the German idealism which preceded it, an idealism whose roots go back to Greek culture and above all to Plato's conception of man. According to Plato the spirit of man was imprisoned in matter and the task of man consisted in surging upward in order to free himself from matter. Matter is actually the nonexistent, while the idea, the mind or spirit, is alone true Being. Man reaches his destiny to the degree that he frees himself from the destruction of matter and lives in the spirit.

There are also other systems which do not hold the spirit alone to be the real and nature the nonexistent, but which rather expect a clarification of Being-as-a-whole to

24

be enacted in man. Occasionally this occurred in the way which was represented by Max Scheler who took the weakness of the spirit over against nature into account, but did so in a way that let spirit put nature at its disposal. By a "cunning of reason" the spirit, which was weak in itself, drew into its service the conative powers of nature by placing before them an objective in the realization of which they do not perceive that they have been overcome.

There is also a development from this spiritual anthropology in which, according to one view, man forgoes the victory of the spirit in the world; instead of this he knows that he is conditioned by nature, that he is prey to senseless historical powers. But there remains for him the possibility of relating himself meaningfully to what is senseless. He is ready to assume this senseless destiny and asserts himself even at his ruin as the rebel, like the defiant Prometheus, against this meaninglessness. Even if he experiences himself as drawn into the Naught he actualizes himself since he is thus prepared to take his futility upon himself and to resist it.

These are tones which we hear from contemporary philosophy and literature, but which we no longer label as "idealistic." In idealism the spirit conquers totally and we have a guarantee of being actualized as spiritual beings, because Being-as-a-whole is spirit. Existentialism, because it is aware of the fragility of such constructions, has renounced this guarantee. It has recognized that in idealism one finds merely the counterpart to that which appears, to existentialism, as naturalism. Whereas in the latter, man is "nothing other than" nature, so in the former he is "nothing other than" spirit. For modern man these buildings and shells of "nothing other than" are smashed; thus unhoused, he is ready to expose the meaningless, the wasteland, by assuming his senseless fate first in order to become authentic and to fulfill his destiny.

THE LIMITS OF ANTHROPOLOGY

Thus we have outlined the two chief stances toward a possible anthropology: the naturalistic-monistic with its fiery denial of the spirit, and, on the other side, the idealistic-dualistic which is ultimately prepared to renounce an idealistic system, but not, however, the self-assertion of the spirit. If we hold them over against each other, we have to conclude that in their special characteristics they must oppose each other and cancel each other out. For naturalism must constantly allow itself to be shown by idealism that it is involved in a self-contradiction when it asserts that man is "nothing other than" nature. For, at the least, this "nothing other than" is still something other than that back to which man can be traced. Conversely, naturalism can correctly oppose self-absolutized idealism by asserting that man consists not only of spirit, and that the victory of spirit can in no way be guaranteed from Being-as-a-whole; and further, that idealism manifests a final desperation of spirit when it is ready to put itself at the mercy of the meaningless. It is appropriate to ask whether man is not betrayed here as well as there where he is conceived only as nature.

Do we not have in this survey of the major types of mythological-religious as well as scientific-philosophical anthropologies a confirmation of our thesis proposed at the outset, namely, that man is just that kind of existent who cannot be systematized? Is it not the case wherever one thinks he has achieved a final answer to the question of man in mythological or scientific form that the mythology is dissolved by science and that the science, if it is reduced to a system, leads itself *ad absurdum?* If man is an existent which can be neither objectified nor systematized, is an anthropology possible at all? Are we not simply dependent upon several pictures which may serve to illumine us, or upon several emergent possibilities which we can grasp? Or does there really exist the possibility of a comprehensive understanding of our existence?

THE AUTHENTIC NATURE OF MAN

If no total view is possible for us we will not be ungrateful for the insights which have resulted from the different fields of anthropological research and reflection, and we shall not conclude that these are only towers of Babel or prisons in which man has become encapsulated and by which his nature has been betrayed. We can arrive at certain conclusions by means of scientific anthropology, whether of the naturalistic or idealistic type. Here we have good reason to mention a special development of scientific anthropology which presents a striking extension of that line in which man appears not so much as a completed product at the summit but in a certain sense as an unfinished existent. It is a peculiarity of contemporary scientific anthropology that it points to the fact that man as a deficient being exhibits a "building plan" (*Bauplan*). It is because man at birth is distinguished from young animals by his lack of development that there is opened to him the possibility of a completely different development. The Basel biologist, Adolf Portmann, has indicated in this connection that man's possibility for culture is essentially based on the fact that he comes into the world in an incomplete condition. While the young animal can immediately help himself in his environment by virtue of his instinct, man at birth is by nature "not yet established," i.e., he cannot help himself and is dependent upon nurture. Therefore he possesses a very special openness to his environment, within which he can—quite differently from the animal—first develop to that form of life to which he seems determined by the peculiarity of the "extra-uterine year of life." Because of his special laws of development man is destined to be more than just

27

another being; he is destined to be that being which must first actualize his being. He does not simply have to follow a law of determinate necessity, as much as he may be entangled in such necessity; rather, through the way in which he understands himself he has to decide what he is.

Modern scientific anthropology knows that the nature of man cannot in advance be scientifically related to a system, and that it cannot generally be said that man is "nothing other than" matter, spirit, life, impulse, or power. Rather, in the way that man understands himself—whether as matter, life, impulse, as a product of economic relationships, as spirit, as a miscarriage of nature, or whatever—he determines in each instance what he is. We each have to elect how we shall understand ourselves. The decision as to how we shall understand ourselves, in which mirror we shall view ourselves, is placed before us precisely by our manifold possibilities which are scientifically neither determinable nor provable.

How do we know our nature? What picture do we select? No one else can decide this for us. Nor can the decision be settled scientifically. Our destiny to freedom and responsibility is evident in this possibility of choice. By accepting our destiny of being that being which in each case has to decide what he will be, we experience the nature of man. Anthropology preserves its character as a science not only by avoiding rigid systematization, but by placing us before the question of our nature, which question we each have to answer as we understand ourselves—and not only by ourselves in isolation, but in the company of those with whom we can understand ourselves to be in such freedom and responsibility. Thus anthropology places us not only before the question "How and in what way do you understand yourself?" It places us as well before the other question, "How do you understand others?"

We find ourselves with science before an ultimate mystery which is not penetrable, but of which we can only speak in the language of myth; namely, that in the infinite expanse of Being a voice rings out, summoning us to responsibility in community, in words like, "Adam, where are you?" and "Cain, where is your brother?" The voice which summons us to responsibility is not to be understood as that of a nameless, silent mystery into which we sink. Rather, it places us before an ultimate ground to which, in the hearing of the voice, we can only ascribe a kind of Being like that which we understand ourselves to be, namely, personhood—Being which resounds with the voice which summons to responsibility and, in this way, to freedom in community. What is this secret of Being which reveals itself to man as Person? Does it perhaps have something to do with that enigmatic sentence at the beginning of the Bible, according to which God created man in his own image, and with the related doctrine of the Apostle Paul that Christ is the image of God and that through him we succeed to divine likeness?

3

Being — The Other Boundary

Being-in-its-totality is the other boundary presented to us in the knowing which takes place within the subject-object scheme, and it is, to be sure, also an absolute rather than a relative boundary. Just as man is ultimately nonobjectifiable, so the world-as-a-whole, the universe, or—abstractly put—Being, cannot be made into an object of knowledge. Being remains in every respect an infinite task for knowledge, a task never to be completed. We have experienced in our time how new dimensions have opened up for research, new dimensions in research on outer space, as well as that of atomic physics on the smallest particles of matter. But there are not only new dimensions and new horizons; for each problem tackled and every new discovery simultaneously confronts research with new problems which call for new solutions. Science experiences its nonfinality because it is never able to grasp Being-in-its totality. That is true not only in a relative sense, but absolutely, because of the finiteness of our minds.

BEING-AS-A-WHOLE AND THE FINITUDE OF MAN

The world as a whole can never become an object for us because our cognitive thinking always presupposes a certain standpoint. The place of knowledge can certainly be changed but never in such a way that all possible places can come into its view at the same time or in a connected continuum. Such a universality would be possible only for the absolute Mind. It is precisely when we engage earnestly in research that we experience the finiteness of our mind. Because our mind is not the world-mind, Being-in-its-totality forms for us the other unconditioned boundary of knowledge.

There are ways of thinking—or better said, of experience—in which the attempt is made to overcome the finiteness of our mind and the incomprehensibility of Being. One of these is by dissolving the finite "I" into the infinite; the other is by letting Being speak to us. The first occurs in the mysticism which seeks to attain an absorption of the finite "I" into the infinite All, that is, into the totality of Being, so that a unity results. Such is the longing of the mystic. But even though he may succeed to this unity at individual moments he cannot make an objective pronouncement about it because he would then objectify that which is not objectifiable. Mysticism, therefore, not only ends in silence but always after waking from the mystical ecstasy finds itself in the emptiness of disappointment.

But instead of the experience in which the "I" sinks into Being, Being can also be personified and thus permitted to speak so that we may hear what rustles and murmurs in its depths and so submit to these powers. We know today to what terrible demons of Being man has fallen victim and what a frightful awakening follows the night of such an episode.

The mystic sinks into the Naught, into Nirvana; and those drunk with history sink into an abyss of the meaninglessness of the event. Here, as well as there, the man who hopes to obtain Being, loses himself in the Naught, that form in which Being discloses itself to him.

COSMOLOGICAL THEORIES AND THE INCONCEIVABILITY OF A
SCIENTIFIC WORLD-PICTURE

Attempts have also been made to grasp Being-in-its-totality in other ways. Take, for example, the science of the world-as-a-whole. Cosmology transmits a picture of the world which is intuited and to which an orientation is possible. World-pictures and world-views are not merely matters of geography. To the world-picture belongs the man who puts himself into it; and the world-view signifies the apprehension of a specific stance within a pictorially conceived world-as-a-whole. From such a world-view the attempt was made originally to reach a world-picture—not merely because of curiosity or thirst for knowledge, but ultimately in order in this way to feel at home in the world and to obtain principles for one's conduct.

It is not surprising that the oldest cosmologies always exhibit a mythological character. Myths are stories about the gods, stories in which gods appear on earth and in which the Eternal is described in temporal forms. The supernatural emerges in the natural sphere. These are projections of human experience in the world into a supra-world by whose forms this world is ordered and made comprehendable.

The oldest cosmologies signify that man wishes to be at home in this uncanny world. He wishes to erect a house and to furnish it. Therefore the heaven arches over the earth like a roof and on it the stars give forth their light and thus by day and night bring order into life. This house also has a cellar, an underworld, and around the whole structure extends a dangerous, primeval sea upon which this three-story house swims. That is a kind of cosmology in which Being-as-a-whole is conceived in mythological form.

Even for the ancient Greeks there were transitions from the pure mythological into scientific cosmology. According to one of these it is recognized that the stars do not revolve around the earth but, as the Pythagoreans held, that the earth, together with other stars, moves around a central fire. As early as 280 B.C. Aristarchus of Samos had already accepted a heliocentric world-picture. Nevertheless, in the periods that followed and during the entire Middle Ages down to the period of the great discoveries, the geocentric world-view of Ptolemy was in vogue chiefly because the church identified herself with this geocentric view. The church not only peopled heaven with God, his angels, and the blessed, but also peopled the underworld with those to be punished, the damned and condemned. Thus men such as Giordano Bruno, Johannes Kepler, and Galileo Galilei had to face enormous resistance from the church when they established, by means of thought and research made possible by new instruments, that old Aristarchus of Samos was, in contrast to Ptolemy, right after all, and when they subsequently expanded this heliocentric world-picture as other systems of suns were discovered.

But even this world-picture of modern astronomy has long since been superseded by modern physics, by the insights of men such as Einstein, Planck, and Heisenberg, whose views may be summarized in four points:

First: Euclidean geometry is valid only for finite space. In infinite space, for example, the sum of the angles of a triangle is no longer equal to two right angles. Therefore, the statement that there can only be one parallel to a line through a point is no longer valid if one is dealing with "curved space." Here presuppositions quite different from those previously assumed hold, and possibilities of a completely new world-picture are opened up.

Second: World-space, although it can be said to be finite, is at the same time unbounded; or vice versa. Although the boundlessness of world-space is established, it means nevertheless that world-space is finite; that is, that there is a spatial end of the world just as the world had a temporal beginning. Modern physicists are seriously concerned with the calculation of the dimensions of world-space and the beginning of the world.

Third: They speak, however, of a universe which is thought to be expanding, and maintain that it came into being possibly as a result of an explosion, or cosmic "big bang."

Fourth: Reliable perception is no longer possible either by laymen or scholars, for as matter is reduced to a mathematical formula, so the world-picture becomes something completely unimaginable. As long as we continue to speak of space and time, extension and angles, these are only models of a reality which is actually no longer imaginable. By overcoming an imaginable world-picture the possibility arises for one that is not imaginable.

Although in this unimaginable world-picture matter is no longer distinguished from spirit, or mind, it is still in vogue to speak, as Aristotle did, of different levels of beings. Thereby a problem which was originally connected with this doctrine of strata arises. As is well known, Aristotle distinguished five levels: first, inorganic, or inanimate; second, the organic in the form of plants which are not merely passive but nourish themselves and continue to grow of themselves; third, animal life which is characterized by free movement, perception, and instinct; fourth, spiritual, or mental, life which belongs to thinking and willing; and fifth, the realm of the divine, the Absolute. Ever since Aristotle proposed this doctrine of levels it has been customary to divide the cosmos into matter, life, soul, and spirit. Some, from Democritus to Ernst Bloch, regard matter as the basic substance to which all others can be traced. Others, like Plato and all subsequent idealists, on the contrary, discern in matter the *Me-on*, the non-existent. For them only the idea is true, and all other substances are only formulations, activities, and developmental forms of the spirit.

Here the problem of unity is evident. How can everything be brought under one common denominator; or—if that is not possible—how can one speak of a unified cosmology? Does not the world decline into a world of matter, a world of life, or of the soul or spirit? Wherein lie the differences between the different levels, and if there are transitions between them how can they be determined? Or if there are fissures between the different levels how is it possible to speak of a unified world-picture?

Because of the objectification of its content a unified, comprehensive world-picture is problematical, and its foundering constantly leads us back to the original philosophical question: Why is there something rather than nothing at all? This is certainly no longer a question of cosmology; rather, this disturbing question, which extends beyond and includes the most daring, most upsetting cosmological theories, is the ontological question. It is the question of Being, i.e., what makes Being Being? The Being of what exists is the object of ontology, the doctrine of Being.

THE ONTOLOGICAL QUESTION AND THE RIDDLE OF BEING

What this is about becomes clear from the different meanings of the little word "is," the verbal form of the substantive, "Being." "Is" serves grammatically as a copula which connects subject and predicate, as, e.g., in the sentence, "The house is large." It expresses something about the "whatness" of the house, about its size. It says something about the nature or essence, to use a more technical word. But the world "is" can also appear in the sentence, "God is." Then it says nothing about the essence of God, about his nature or being, but about his existence, that he is.

35

One asks in ontology, "What is Being? Is it essence (*Sosein*) or existence (*Dasein*)?" These are questions which occupied not only Greek ontology but medieval ontology as well. They have been revived in our time with a new force, when, for example, Sartre can summarize his philosophy in the sentence, "L'existence précède l'essence" ("existence precedes essence"). The decision about this question has enormous consequences which indicate that ontology, of all considerations, is not a purely abstract, theoretical business. The question penetrates into the self-understanding of man and asks whether ontology is not ultimately an expression of the specifically human self-understanding.

Today, over against the newly awakened interest of philosophy and theology in these ontological questions, there stands the perspective which appeared with Kant, namely, that in our cognition we do not have to do with Being as it is in itself but with Being as it appears to us. Why then do we speak of Being, essence, and existence, as if we had to do with Being-in-itself rather than with its appearances? In his criticism of ontology Kant appealed to the notion that in our theoretical statements we are always only dealing with Being as knowable in the intuitive forms of space and time and in the categories of our understanding. But this philosophy of consciousness should be asked what Being signifies for it, if it has to do only with phenomena. It is understandable that a philosopher interested in ontology, like Martin Heidegger, concludes that for Kant the word "is" meant only the "position" of a certain essence. The philosophy of consciousness, with its thesis of the phenomenality of Being, cannot really do justice to the question of the riddle of Being, certainly not if—contrary to Kant—it would like to regard Being as posited by thinking.

The question of Being is precisely that question over

against which we cannot stand as spectator and judge. Rather in it there emerges before us an abyss which threatens to engulf us. It takes the breath away from the one who takes it seriously because therein he experiences himself as expelled into the Naught as if into a vacuum. Heidegger was not the first to perceive this, for Kant was already aware of it when he allowed the highest Being, which can say to itself, "I am from eternity to eternity, and outside me there is nothing save by my will," to pose the question for itself, "But whence then am I?" only to continue, "Here everything sinks below us, and the greatest perfection, like the least, is suspended without moorings before the speculative reason which expends no effort to prevent the disappearance of either."[1] Speculation may camouflage the Naught with which we are confronted in the question of Being, but it cannot fill the emptiness. It is precisely the critical thinking of consciousness, remaining conscious of its boundaries, which disperses the fog in which ontology would like to engulf us—even that of the Heideggerian "thinking of Being."

COSMOGONIC THINKING AND BIBLICAL FAITH IN CREATION

The oldest attempt, however, to master the uncanniness of the question of the why of Being—older even than cosmology and ontology—is cosmogonic thinking. Cosmogony means the "genesis of the world." The oldest myths begin with a presentation of the origin of the world. In this way they attempt to answer the question "Why is there something and not nothing?" In order to overcome the shock of this question, to fill in the emptiness or the Naught into which it flows, stories are told of the origin of all things. In this way the world becomes conceivable.

---

[1] Immanuel Kant, *Critique of Pure Reason,* trans. Norman Kemp Smith (New York: St. Martin's Press, 1965) , pp. 513 ff.

Even as early as 1000 B.C. an ancient hymn of the Rigveda Epic narrated that, in the beginning when there was neither earth nor heaven, air nor gods, there was only one who breathed. From that one the world came into being. But that took place so long ago that even the gods do not know about it; it is known only to Him-Who-Sees-All. But even he does not know whether the world was created or not. Around 800 B.C. Hesiod explained how earth and heaven originated out of Chaos and Night. Heaven impregnated the earth and from this union the gods emerged and began their struggle with each other. In the course of this story men finally emerge to people the earth.

Or we can think of the biblical myth of the story of creation, which can be traced back to the Babylonian story about Marduk who pierced the primeval dragon Tiamat with a spear and formed the earth out of her. Similarly, in the biblical story of creation God overcomes the primeval flood, chaos (in whose Hebraic name "Tehom" the Babylonian "Tiamat" still resounds), and so causes the earth and its inhabitants to emerge. This happens no longer by means of a deadly struggle but by the word which God speaks.

The Christian doctrine of the creation of the world out of nothing at the beginning of time rests on this myth. But for this purpose the biblical story of creation is possibly unsuited for it does not mention the beginning of time or of the Naught. The myth, rather, presupposes that the primeval chaos is already present before creation; thus theology makes of this chaos the Naught, so as to avoid the implication that God is the creator of the chaos. For this reason the Bible is unaware of the question which is made so much of in theology, the question of whether creation took place before or in time. Theology employs the myth not only to solve this philosophical question but also as a description of the first historical act of the God whose assistance Israel experienced in its history over against powers which it saw embodied in the myth of the struggle with the dragon.

In view of the philosophical problem connected with the doctrine of *creatio ex nihilo,* as well as of the difficulties which are bound up with its dependence upon the doctrine of the revelatory character of Scripture, it is not surprising that in the modern era, in place of the doctrine of creation, there has emerged the conception of the development of Being according to immanent laws. This conception no longer has any room for an intervention of God and no longer needs such an hypothesis for its explanation. In this theory of evolution there is no concern with an explanation as to how the world originated, but only with how it achieved its present form and will possibly develop. In place of the doctrine of a beginning of the world through the creation of God, which is untenable for this evolutionary cosmogony, it has introduced the conception of the eternity of the world as was held in the philosophy of antiquity—a conception which has long stood as the opposite of the biblical-Christian doctrine of creation. It is beyond doubt that the doctrine of the eternity of the world and the doctrine of the world as created present two quite different conceptions, so different as to be mutually exclusive. The eternity of the world permits no creation at the beginning of the world and creation excludes an eternal existence of the world.

The difficulties which accrue to faith in creation because of its mythological form, the problem of a beginning of time, and, as well, the inconsistency of its appeal to Scripture—these difficulties weaken this faith's case before reason. But if evolutionism takes stock of itself, the result would be that it presses toward that concept of the Naught which has played such a problematic role in the

Christian doctrine of creation. This could happen in such a way that this concept of the Naught will become more important as a designation for an unavoidable state of affairs, the awareness of which leads to a new understanding of the idea of creation.

THE CONFRONTATION WITH THE NAUGHT

Science confronts the Naught where it becomes aware of the boundaries of knowledge. We have recognized one such boundary to be Being-in-its-totality. Does not evolutionism press toward this boundary when it dispenses with an explanation of the origin of Being and assumes the eternity of the world? Eternity is something which cannot be imagined or conceived—otherwise it would not be eternity. For objectifying thinking eternity is like a Naught. This Naught, of the inconceivable, surrounds the realms of what we know, as in the old myths the primeval sea circumscribes the earth. Science has only to perceive its boundary in order to press toward the Naught. And if it exceeds these limits it encounters difficulties in the insoluble problems in which it gets entangled—difficulties which in their indeterminability are not inferior to the monsters which inhabit the mythological sea.

But then the scientist encounters the Naught not merely on the perimeters of his sphere of knowledge and of knowledge as such but also in his own finiteness which announces itself to him in the ineluctability of the end which stands before him. Here he confronts not merely a Naught which announces itself to him in individual places, like the boundaries of knowledge and its sphere, of which—if he is clever—he takes account in his thinking and in the evaluation of his results. But this Naught no longer affords him the possibility to be content within its boundaries and to settle there. This Naught, which looms before us in our death, devours even the possibility of such cleverness in that it abolishes all Being of which man—without disregarding his limits—could make a pronouncement.

But how inconsequential are all these cosmologies, ontologies, and cosmogonies in view of this end which devolves upon idealist and materialist alike, upon believer and unbeliever, the one who hopes and the one who doubts! The distinctive characteristic of man certainly consists in the fact that he can be aware of this end and therefore need not simply die like an animal but can appropriate this end in his thinking. But even this anticipation of death in abandonment to this Naught does not mean an overcoming of the Naught but more than ever an awareness of it. Let us suppose that this Naught which looms before us in this premonition of death should come to signify something else to each of us, according to the manner in which we frame this experience of being abandoned into the Naught; death still remains death. And even if that which we have thought about Being be extended to others, it still remains true that he who now thinks will someday no longer exist.

In this awareness of the fact that in the future it is unavoidable that we shall cease to exist, we encounter the Naught in its most radical form. In this radical disclosure of our destiny of death it envelops all the ways in which we attempt to explain it and in which we express or attempt to overcome our anxiety about it.

It is precisely at this point that we find the origin of all mythical cosmogonies, philosophical ontologies, and even the cosmologies of science. Because they attempt to solve the question of Being, which is concerned with the origin and nature of Being-in-itself, the question "Why is there something rather than nothing?" continually announces itself in them as an ultimate, insoluble riddle. And thus they unavoidably present us with this question.

41

EXISTENCE AS GRACE

Whatever is, perishes. But even in the perishing there *is* that which perishes. In perishing there is Being. So long as there is perishing in Being, it is not nothing—it is Being. In the face of the Naught we know about Being. We ourselves are in this world. As it does not exist for me apart from my being, so it is given to me in conjunction with my being as the time and space of the realization of this my being in Being. Cosmologies, ontologies, and cosmogonies are attempts to orient us to this situation in which we find ourselves, so that we shall fulfill rather than miss the meaning of our being. They perform this service for us when they enable us to be "at home" in Being, and, with respect to the Naught which constantly surrounds and threatens us, to know Being and its particular possibilities as a gift, that is, as an opportunity to be grasped and actualized at every moment, as grace. As a designation for the possibility of Being, which in light of the Naught does not stand at our disposal but is given to us, "grace" is the most appropriate term, describing as it does the fact of our being situated in the Being surrounded by the Naught. Being in face of the Naught is grace. Because it enables us to fulfill the destiny of the moment it alone deserves the name of eternity. Eternity occurs there where the significance of the moment becomes clear to us—whether as judgment or blessedness. In such moments we experience what creation is, namely, to be blessed with creaturely existence, and we begin to suspect why in several passages of the New Testament the first creation is connected with the Christ.

4

Thinking and Faith in God

Let us recall briefly some of the steps which we have taken so far on this journey to a thinking faith. We began with the nature of cognition, which consists in the fact that a knowing subject stands over against an object which is known or to be known. Cognition always takes place in this relation of subject and object. There is no cognition without a subject and an object. A subject is necessary to enact the knowing. Even when technical instruments are employed someone has to be there to program the apparatus and utilize the results. It is thus never the case—as certain conceptions of Being attempt to claim—that Being enacts thought. Just as knowing is determined by that which borders it and Being has to announce itself to us, it is nevertheless we who enact the knowing. But the object of knowledge cannot simply be dissolved into a product of the subject. Knowing is never a purely subjective event even though the object of knowledge is formed by the knowing.

It is a task of knowing to distinguish fantasy from reality. Knowing is a matter of objectivity, of the universal provability of the interrelations of things which exist. Therefore all knowing must take into account the subjective limitation—whether to eliminate it if possible or appropriately to utilize it—because there are objects of knowledge whose nature we are able to grasp only if we consciously and subjectively participate in them. Whether subjectivity is eliminated or utilized, the purpose is the same, namely, the univocal designation of states of affairs. This process of cognition is indeed inconclusive and ultimately always remains relative. The essence of scientific methods, whether those of the realm of the humanities or of the natural sciences, consists in the knowledge of this inconclusiveness and relativity. In contradistinction to every kind of dogmatism science knows its boundaries and its relativity, even though it can attain to demonstrative and objective knowledge within its own systems and perspectives.

In its legitimate struggle constantly to expand the horizon of its knowledge, science confronts two quantities which are never ultimately conceivable, not even in a relative sense, and which because they are not objectifiable prove themselves initially and from then on more clearly still to be elusive to the grasp of knowledge. These are, first, the *self* which executes the act of knowing and which ultimately cannot "see" itself because this self always becomes what it will be by the way in which it understands itself. And second, the *object-world-in-its-totality* which may become an object of science only partially and in some of its aspects.

There are two realities which because of their peculiarities cannot become objects of scientific knowledge: man, whose nature is not determined but is to be actualized only in man's own self-understanding; and Being, which in its totality eludes our grasp and which we become aware of at the boundaries of our particular knowledge. The knowledge of these boundaries of our knowledge is a knowledge of a special sort. It provides us with no new information but allows everything which is objectively knowable to be seen in a special light. Man is always something other than that which he knows himself to be. To him it is unavoidable that he either is or will become what he understands himself to be. Similarly, Being-as-a-whole could be objectified only by the absolute Mind, or Spirit. It is a concern of our finite mind to know of these two absolute boundaries in addition to all relative ones. This critical self-knowledge of thinking—with respect both to its possibilities and its boundaries—signifies not a quantitative increase of knowledge but a qualitative modification of all knowledge and of the knower himself. It effects an awareness of our responsible personhood within the sphere of the mystery of Being, an awareness which is no longer objectifiable but is enacted in all our knowledge within the inevitable subject-object scheme.

From the perspective of this consciousness of our responsible personhood the various anthropologies can no longer be said to increase our knowledge of the object, Man. It is rather the case that we encounter in them the expressive forms of the ways in which man understands himself. They are thus testimonies and confessions of his personhood—which is something quite different from whatever can be said objectively. These forms of man's self-understanding are encompassed by Being-as-a-whole, for any self-understanding which occurs belongs to Being.

It is precisely because of this anthropological element that Being-as-a-whole first discloses that it is not objectively and finally knowable. Nevertheless, doctrines of the world and of Being are necessary and useful attempts to become oriented to the possibilities of Being and to avoid getting lost in their infinitude. Perhaps we can structure Being as a shell in which we—preserved from uncanniness—attempt meaningfully to structure our own existence. But this shell of Being, which we technically and in our thoughts furnish in such a cozy way, has an uncanny affinity—whether regarded cognitively or experientially—with the Naught: cognitively, because Being-in-its-totality eludes our grasp when we attempt to grasp it conceptually; experientially, because Being-in-its-totality remains for us an empty concept since we are not at all able to fill in the concept from our experience. For our knowledge Being-in-its totality is the Naught, the abyss out of which all objects emerge and into which they sink. Experientially this proximity of Being and the Naught, this uncanny transition from Being into the Naught, consists in the fact that our existence, with respect to what concerns us ultimately, is determined by our frailty. Every moment of our existence founders on the abyss of the Naught. What is the meaning of Being-in-death? Does anxiety about the end of existence perhaps know more about the nature of Being than all knowledge of individual existents, more than all world-systems which encompass heaven and earth, time and eternity? Does the anxiety which is fearful before the Naught but cannot explain its fear know more about the mystery of Being than all sciences and all constructions of world-views which wish to dispel this anxiety?

Man who experiences himself abandoned into the Naught perceives even in his impotence a power which summons him to responsibility. This is a power which places man's existence at his own disposal, as that realm of Being assigned to him for the actualization of responsible life. We designate as *faith* the act of becoming aware of this situation in which we become conscious of our responsibility and of the mystery of Being and through which consciousness we come to ourselves. Although this is a situation which is no longer objectifiable, it can be clarified only by means of objective thinking. For such faith, Being is grace, in that it gives to man the possibility of actualizing this responsibility which constitutes his essence.

THE ESSENCE AND PHENOMENAL WORLD OF FAITH

In this way we have come by means of thought into that realm which encounters us in the world of religious phenomena as faith. Faith in a religious sense comprises not only the pronouncements but also the practices in which man—moved by the question of the meaning of his existence—struggles to order, assure, and structure his life with respect to ultimate powers, thus participating in life's fulfillment. Faith deals with that to which man in his existence experiences himself as related, the ultimate powers not at his disposal. These are powers which he attempts to utilize for his own salvation or which he desires to serve for the same purpose. Both of these encounter us in the historical forms of faith: the attempt to get control of these powers and thereby secure oneself with respect to them; and conversely, the struggle to throw oneself upon them, surrender to them, serve them, and praise them in thought and deed.

The phenomenal world of faith is infinite and confronts us in past and present in various forms. These forms are altered by great and small reformations, which stamp the history in which the forms emerge, struggle with each other, undergo change, vanish, and reemerge in a new form. This phenomenal world of faith, which forms the object of the science and history of religion, is enormously manifold and, despite all similarities, encompasses the greatest opposites which mutually exclude each other. It reaches from the forms of superstition and magic to the highest forms of spiritual religion in which the gods and demons are dissolved into the ineffable All-One, in which the babble of human voices from the world, the beyond, and the heart makes place for an ultimate silence in which temples decay and in which even faith annuls itself for the sake of its own purity. Precisely in this process of self-purification can faith reemerge in an altered form either by abandoning the traditional or by appropriating it in a different way.

Faith deals basically with what has previously been our concern, namely, with cognition and its boundaries: man, Being, and the Naught. Cognition is its concern insofar as faith is understood as a knowing which is delimited from other, profane knowledge. Apart from this secret announcement and revelation man could not know about his salvation. Natural knowledge seems to be circumscribed by a knowledge from secret, supernatural sources which are concerned with the ultimate questions of human existence and of Being as such. The Holy Scriptures tell of the origin of man, his nature, his possible Fall, and his redemption and consummation. But they also speak of the origin of the world, its future, and the powers ruling in it. The Scriptures know about the secret of the world and about the Naught which surrounds and threatens it; but they also know about the salvation which consists in the conquest of anxiety before the Naught and in the overcoming of the destructive chaos in life and in the world. The Scriptures report such things in the form of myth rather than in a scientific way because myth corresponds to the nature of an appropriate discourse about such things. As we have seen, man and Being-in-its-totality are not objectifiable in terms of scientific knowledge. We can appropriately and ultimately speak of ourselves and of the world in which we find ourselves only by seeking beyond what is objectifiable for a reality which when we become authentic occurs as the grace of Being against the background of the Naught. Statements about man and the world are ultimately statements of faith, that is, statements of our self-understanding which makes use of objectifying conceptuality but which is not itself objectifiable in its enactment. The objective pronouncements of our understanding of ourselves and the world point to the nonobjectifiable relationship of ourselves and the world to Transcendence. Only in its appearance is this relationship to Transcendence a scientific matter. It is enacted, however, in the thinking of faith which in its objectivity inquires beyond these appearances and is thus open for the language of Transcendence.

Man is indeed not man if he has not learned that he is summoned to responsibility and that he can miss the meaning of his existence if it does not dawn upon him that eternity is something more than a time which extends indefinitely backwards and forwards. Eternity is rather that moment in which man becomes aware of the mystery of Being, a mystery consisting in the fact that he experiences himself as destined for personhood and that the possibility of its realization is grace.

THE ROLE OF THINKING IN THE HISTORY OF FAITH

If what we are discussing is not to remain an abstract discourse but become meaningful for us, to summon and reach us and show us the way, how could it happen otherwise than that the gods and their messengers, saints and saviors, encounter us and draw us into the sphere of this event? It is for this reason that the mythical tradition is the most appropriate language for the reality of faith. To this mythical language there corresponds cultic practice and personal participation in its enactment. It constitutes the greatness and the weakness of conceptual thinking that it can direct us to the reality of faith, but because of the explanatory function of its own objectivity cannot surrender to the participation of which it speaks. On the contrary, in cultic practice and personal piety there can occur what we understand as the relationship of responsible existence to Transcendence. Here we do not merely stand over against this reality, but are admitted into it, i.e., it becomes an event in our lives.

Cultic practices and religious forms of life indeed offer objectifications in which salvation is mediated and in which it can therefore be distorted into sorcery and magic. But the cult is not characterized merely by these objective forms, such as the correct preaching of the word of God and the correct execution of the sacraments within which, if done properly, salvation will occur. The reception of salvation always presupposes personal participation, which of course does not exclude the activity of preaching and sacrament. Although at this point the various historical forms of faith are basically divided in their understanding of cultic practice, it can nonetheless be said that as a result of participation in the cult and as a result of personal religious life it is expected that man will become quite different from what he was previously, and that there will occur the experience of becoming authentic, the experience about which faith is concerned. Salvation becomes reality only in appropriation and, to be sure, only in personal responsibility.

In this sense, thinking can serve to clarify the nature of faith, and it is well known that it has played a large role in the history of faith. The overcoming of the Greek mysteries and cults of the city-state with their Hesiodic and Homeric pantheon took place through the early Greek thinkers who replaced this world of divinities with an omnicompetent divine principle, or God himself. Even in the history of the Christian faith thinking has played a great role, as is also true of the religions of China and, more especially, India. It is as difficult to separate faith from thinking in these high religions as in medieval theology. "That old harlot reason" is an invention of the quite unphilosophical mentality of Luther. But the mention of this reformer points up to us the tensions which can emerge in relating thinking and faith and which from time to time have emerged. It is not incorrect to say that the God of the thinker is usually different from the God of traditional faith. There are formulations of thought and forms of faith which only reveal their differences, and there are, in the two spheres, few indications that thinking can become believing, or faith thinking, without betraying their distinctiveness. Criticism can unmask superstition but even a thinking which absolutizes itself is superstition. Superstition is not at all confined to the realm of the religious. It can also emerge in the garb of science. And in both extremes we have the opposite of a thinking faith.

We wish to clarify this relation of thinking and faith by means of an example which is significant within the history of thought as well as faith, namely, the question of the proofs for the existence of God. From time to time thinkers have arisen in opposition to faith in God because they judged the ideas about God to be products of an uncritical thinking. But time and again there have also been thinkers positively concerned with proofs for the existence of God. One may indeed ask which of the two groups has rendered a better service to faith in God, the atheists or the apologists. Just as there is a deaf atheism, so there is an offensive apologetic. From the great number of arguments for the existence of God which have emerged in the history of our problem, we shall attempt to deal only with the five which are most important.

THE FIVE SO-CALLED PROOFS OF THE EXISTENCE OF GOD

First, there is the cosmological argument, which attempts to prove the existence of God from the existence of the world. The world would not be here, so it is argued, unless it had a cause. Just as each individual thing has its cause, so the totality must have a cause, and the primordial cause of all things, the *prima causa*, the first cause, is God.

But then the divine origin is to be inferred not only from the facticity of the world but also from the *how*. The second or physico-theological, or teleological, proof consists in arguing for God from the way in which the world is constituted. "Physico-theological" means that God is to be proven from the natural character of the world; "teleological" means what is directed toward a purpose or goal. The purposeful arrangement and the richness of meaningful relationships, both great and small, could not be merely the consequence of an atomic explosion or an accident. The wise arrangement of the world discloses its All-wise Creator.

But in the world there is evil as well as good. However, even in this knowledge of good and evil some perceive a further proof. Why does man know about good and evil? Why does his conscience speak to him? From what source do we know about righteousness? From the existence of this moral consciousness is inferred a highest moral Lawgiver and Judge. This moral argument is the third proof.

Fourthly, there is the religio-historical argument for God's existence. Is there a people without religion, without a faith in supernatural powers, without some ideas about what lies beyond? This whole world of the religious cannot be simply an illusion. Something in it has to correspond to reality.

While the arguments previously mentioned proceed from concrete phenomena like the existence and constitution of the world from the conscience and the facts of religion, a fifth argument is confident that it can derive the reality of God from the concept of God alone. God—what else could that be but the most perfect Being? How could he be the most perfect Being if he lacked existence? In that case something would prevent his perfection. Therefore: If by definition God is the most perfect Being, then he must also exist. Such is the ontological proof.

Such mental operations have often been utilized by

faith for the sake of its facade or substructure, while for its most important doctrines it has customarily appealed to revelation. But in these proofs of the existence of God, which are supposedly plausible for thinking, faith still saw the possibility of persuading unbelievers or of preparing for the deeper insights of revelation.

Thinking resorted to the proofs of God's existence, however, mostly because the traditional faith had become problematical. Although previous ideas and institutions could no longer be accepted, the attempt was made, because of their accepted meaning, to inquire whether or not something true lay behind them. And thus it was thought possible to discover the truth of faith by means of the cosmological, physico-theological, moral, religio-historical, and ontological arguments. In this way exactly the same mistake was made as in the religious tradition which had been abandoned. The charge was made that revelation had been used as if it were present objectively in one church or in one sacred tradition. These rejected institutions and traditions were now, however, replaced with mental operations, that is, with rational insights in which the same objectivity—now naturally rather than supernaturally established—made the claim to be universally valid. These rational proofs which emerged in place of dogmas showed themselves to be no less fragmentary and problematic than the dogmas they were to replace.

THE PROBLEMATIC CHARACTER OF THE ARGUMENTS FOR GOD

Take the case of the cosmological argument as an example: Can a cause be demonstrated for everything? Certainly in the world—but not beyond it. What we assume to be the cause of the existence of the world has already become a part of this world due to the fact that we call it the first cause (*Ur-sache*). In our world of objects this first cause must also have its cause and so this quest for a *prima causa* leads to an infinite regress. For objective thinking there can be no such thing as a first cause. The question founders on the incomprehensibility of Being-in-its-totality.

What happens if we disregard the mere fact of the world's existence and in its place turn our attention to its essential characteristics, as happens in the physico-theological, or teleological, argument? Do not the meaningfulness and purposefulness of the world, by which some seek to find a special proof for the existence of God, become problematical as a result of opposite experiences? In our lifetime abysses have yawned before us which cause us to speak of the enigmatical character of the world. How is a good God to be inferred from such a world? Is he not more likely to be the opposite of good? There is good reason for the fact that the history of religion is replete with grotesque devils. To us they also seem to correspond to a reality.

The conscience, furthermore, does not speak universally in the same way. Through which conscience does God speak, if right and wrong, good and evil can be so differently conceived? Is it true that world history is world judgment? Does good always prevail? Is the world morally so structured that a moral Lawgiver can be inferred from it? Does not the course of world history give us reason to deny God? Are the diabolic and the evil compatible with faith in God's goodness and perfection?

Any religion that asserts this could also be a priestly fraud or an invention of the strong who wished in this way to suppress the weak. Is religion's power exhausted only by the fact that, as has often been said, it satisfies our needs? How can one prove that it is not an illusion? Was not Calvin somewhat correct when he declared that religion is nothing more than an idol factory?[1] Does not much in the phenomenal world of faith—even in Calvin's faith—confirm this judgment?

---

[1] John Calvin, *Institutes of the Christian Religion,* Book I, Chapter 11.

The ontological argument is also deprived of its foundation by such doubt. It would be valid only if Being corresponds to thinking. Kant remarked in this connection that a hundred mental dollars are not a hundred real dollars.[2] God is no more the most perfect being if I think him to be such than I possess a hundred dollars if I think about it. What is thought can prove to be an illusion.

The conventional arguments for the existence of God raise grave problems. With them we are no better off than with certain religious superstitions. In both we have to do with transgressions of the boundary for the purpose of laying hold on what is nonobjectifiable and bringing it under the aegis of a religion, a cult, or some kind of speculation. It is always a betrayal of thinking if it engages itself in a proof of God. Genuine faith has absolutely no need of such questionable proofs. Thinking and faith are truly much differently related than in these delusive undertakings.

GOD AS A PERSON FOR PERSONAL EXISTENCE

Before we opened up this problem of the arguments for the existence of God the appropriate relationship of thinking and faith had been clarified. That took place where we came up against the factor of our personal responsibility which connects man with Being. That we are responsible we can prove neither to ourselves nor to others. I can only know myself to be responsible or act responsibly. Then I know with what it deals, namely with Being or Not-being. I obliterate myself as a person if I do not perceive my responsibility; and I actualize myself in no other way than by taking upon myself my responsibility. I can only ask another person, "Have you not noticed that it is a concern of yours to be responsible?" But I cannot demonstrate this responsibility to him. I can only make him aware of the way in which he can prove his responsibility to himself

---

[2] Immanuel Kant, op. cit., p. 505.

and of what being irresponsible means for him. But we become aware of what responsibility is only by accepting and enacting it. In this way we become participants in the grace of Being which frees us from the arbitrariness into which all objective Being dissolves if we wish to lay hold of it and place ourselves in its custody. Precisely in the abyss of the Naught which opens before us, unconditionality is manifest in our conditionality, eternity in time.

To the same degree that hearing the call to responsibility is our affair, so its implementation does not lie in our power. It comes to us as a surprise, just as God in the mythical stories surprised men with his summons with which they must struggle and through the obedience or disobedience of which either salvation or judgment occurred. These are such events that can only be spoken of in signs, gestures, pictures, and symbols, and which can be understood, as the Apostle Paul says, only "out of faith into faith."

Two examples may serve to illustrate what is involved here. The first stems from the seventeenth century and concerns the great French mathematician and physicist, Blaise Pascal, who confessed, "The eternal silence of these infinite spaces makes me shudder."[3] This same man, who knew the boundaries of that which formed the object of his research, carried on his person to his death a slip of paper, wrapped in parchment and sewn into his garment. On this piece of paper the experience of a certain night, dated exactly, "The year of grace, 1654, Monday the 23rd of November," was given in stammering words. Following the names of the saints of this day, one reads: "From about 10:30 P.M. until about half an hour after midnight—Fire—God of Abraham, God of Isaac, God of Jacob, not of the philosophers and scholars—Certainty, Certainty—Feeling, Joy, Peace—God of Jesus Christ— Your God is my God—The world and everything forgot-

---

[3] *Pensées*, No. 206.

THINKING AND FAITH IN GOD

ten except God—Only on the way the Gospel teaches is
He to be found—Greatness of the human soul—Joy, Joy,
Joy—Tears of Joy—I have separated myself from
Him—My God, why hast Thou forsaken me?—May I
never be separated from Him."[4]

This so-called "Memorial," from which we have cited
several passages, was not meant for publication. Nevertheless we can conclude from it that there was for Pascal
something beyond that God of the philosophers and scien-
tists which made his inquiring mind shudder, namely, the
God of Abraham, Isaac, and Jacob. This is the God of his
faith by which he lived in his church—though under
attack by it—in whose cult he participated, and whose personal revelation filled him with joy and certainty.

To this can be added the testimony of the faith of
another thinker, this one from our own time. It is the
Jewish philosopher of religion, Martin Buber, who in his
work *Begegnungen* once wrote two sentences which are
very significant for our case: "If believing in God means
being able to speak of him in the third person, then I do
not believe in God. If believing in God means being able
to speak to him, then I believe in God."[5]

The first statement—speaking of God in the third person—is for faith something like the Fall of man, for such
discourse thinks that in its objectivity it can be like God.
The second—speaking to God—means, conversely and in
its reference to what is nonobjectifiable, the reality of God
for the one who prays. Prayer is the only appropriate discourse with respect to God, for it is a talking to, not about,
God. For the one praying the reality of God is no problem—otherwise he would not pray but would reflect upon
the possibility of prayer. But what for thought always
remains a mere possibility—even an impossible possibility—in prayer becomes reality itself!

---

[4] *Mémorial de Pascal.*
[5] Stuttgart: Kohlhammer, 1960, p.

57

5

Faith and Ethical Norms

There is no thinking without objects but there are objects of thought which are not merely objects, for they point to what is not objectifiable, namely, to responsible personhood which cannot be objectified; to Being-in-its-totality which we are not able fully to grasp; and to Transcendence for personal existence which cannot be universally proven. It is the function of the "practical reason," rather than the "theoretical," to speak concretely and practically of the possibility of personhood and its loss, of the grace of Being and confrontation with the Naught, of God who speaks to us and is not silent like the Naught. The thinking which deals with the ultimately unthinkable is not a musing, not an indulging in unreal things; rather, this thinking has to do precisely with what is concrete and practical. It is a genuinely practical thinking. It has to do with the objects which in their entirety form the world and it stands in constant relationship to them, even if it is concerned with something other than these objectivities. The nonobjectifiable dimension of personhood, of Being in its mystery, and of the transcendence of both, is flashed upon the things of this world, just as the self-actualization of personhood occurs in this world. In this manner the world becomes a situation for me, that is, a specific sphere of this world achieves for me a specific significance as the

58

space and time of the realization of my personhood. As unworldly as personhood is, it nevertheless occurs in the world. If we designate faith as the ultimate relatedness of personal existence to its Transcendence, to the voice which summons it to responsibility, and also understand such faith as self-realization and its parallel forming of the world, even then what is at stake is something highly practical. That kind of thinking by which man becomes aware both of himself as a person and of a personal power summoning him to responsibility is no mere theoretical thinking. It reaches beyond the boundary-experiences of its objectification in our inwardness and in its relatedness to Transcendence into what is practical. It consists, then, in unconditioned inner acts of personal decision and choice in concrete situations. My situation, in which I by choosing actualize myself as a responsible person in unconditioned decisions, is no abstraction, for it is determined by a host of concrete things and relationships in which it is involved. Just as my personal existence is no theory, the same can be said for what is unconditioned. Unconditionedness occurs in the enactment of my self-actualization as person and, if it succeeds, is experienced as summons and grace in a highly personal concretion.

CO-HUMANITY

It is not to be overlooked in this connection that, in this enactment of the actualization of my personhood, I am never alone as a person in a situation, standing over against God, but am always together with other persons. Here is the place, therefore, at which we must call attention to the sphere of co-humanity. The other person, to be sure, as a "Thou," belongs to my personhood. I can treat a person as an object, as a mere "It," and not hear the claim which he makes on me as a "Thou." Then I deny to him what I claim for myself. Personhood, which can be actualized only together with other persons, directs us toward others. Therefore speech belongs to human existence.

We can use language merely as an informational aid for our orientation, as a kind of self-assertion. It can, however, make accessible to us the possibility of experiencing the other person as a "Thou"—something which can happen in no other way than through the special communicative instrument of language because its enables us not only to explain and prove but to understand and enjoy personal community as well.

This personhood of the other, to which we here call attention with such emphasis, also plays a role in ultimate relatedness to Transcendence. If this relationship to Transcendence does not end in the silence of the Naught or in a sinking into the abyss, and we encounter the voice which calls us to responsibility, then with the use of terms like "voice," "summons," "summoned to responsibility" we are moving at the same time into the sphere of co-humanity from which they are drawn and to which they point. God is the great "Thou" about whom I do not know unless I know this "Thou" within the co-human sphere. Prayer is the application of an experience of human personhood in community to Transcendence.

In the phenomenal world we meet things which wish to be respected by us as persons. As we fail ourselves if we do not actualize ourselves as persons, if we lose ourselves in things, even so we cannot attain to the goal of personhood unless we concede the same goal to others and help them to actualize it by encountering them as "Thou's" rather than as "It's." Even with respect to this co-humanity thinking assumes a practical form. It is actualized in our concrete attitude and conduct toward our fellowmen who make the claim to be persons.

With this thinking, which is directed to the realization of ourselves and our fellowmen, we find ourselves in the sphere of ethics, for ethics is reflection upon the appropriateness of human acts—in individuals as well as in communities. It deals with the correct action by which I become genuine with others and through which salvation is actualized in community. In this sphere the categories of good and evil are added to the previously employed categories of right and wrong, true and false, open and hidden.

THE INTERRELATEDNESS AND FINITENESS OF THE FOUR CONTRASTS ESSENTIAL TO THE CONCEPTION OF THE ETHICAL

We speak of right and wrong in the context of objective knowledge. Rightness and wrongness can within certain limits be demonstrated objectively but never with ultimate validity. The judgment true or false, to the contrary, refers not to our conceptual knowledge but to the actualization of our personhood. Therefore it is not universally and objectively demonstrable. As Plato said in his Seventh Epistle, truth occurs between friends in good hours.[1] Truth occurs when personhood is actualized. The distinction between open and hidden, finally, pertains to the relatedness of faith to Transcendence. Transcendence can conceal itself, so that we—like Pascal—"shudder before the infinite, eternal silence of infinite spaces"; or it can happen that we hear the voice which summons us to responsibility with the words, "I am the Lord, your God."

The fourth category, good and evil, refers to our acts, to the will to realize our personhood in community. Good and evil are qualifications of ethical thinking and activity. The behavior of a person toward himself and others, the thoughts on which this behavior is grounded and justified, and the implementation of its acts are not merely right or wrong, true or mendacious, but are, rather, good or evil.

The relationship in which these four categories stand to

---

[1] *The Seventh Letter,* 341c.

each other—right-wrong, true-false, open-hidden, and good-evil—is highly significant for the comprehension of the meaning of good and evil. Each of these four distinctions has its special peculiarity but they nevertheless all stand in relation to each other. Therefore we must call to mind the nature of the first three distinctions in order to develop constructively the nature of good and evil.

The designations "right and wrong" refer to judgments in the sphere of theoretical-objective thinking. "Right," or "correct," as the qualification of a judgment publicly designates something in a conceptually univocal way. As scientific knowledge, this kind of thinking forms the foundation of the essential sphere of all thinking concerned with clarity—even the ethical. We use the concepts of objective thinking and seek to distinguish right from wrong by means of univocal terms. The significance and worth of this objective thinking lies in the fact that it rises above mere opinion, personal notions, and fantastic indulgence in worlds of images, and subjects everything to its categories of right and wrong. But we should not forget that such knowledge is limited and inconclusive. In this sphere only objects of knowledge which constantly remain relative are possible.

Both the possibilities and the boundaries of objective knowledge are to be taken into account when we deal with good and evil. We can speak of good and evil only if we designate univocally what we mean and sharply distinguish between right and wrong. But if they are to be related to the realm of the personal and to Transcendence, good and evil are never to be conceived merely in this theoretical way. It should not be overlooked that conceptual thinking has its boundaries precisely in the comprehension of good and evil possible for it. As indispensable as is the conceptualizing of good and evil, nevertheless, the personhood to be actualized and also the personhood of another are not conceptually conceivable. Good and evil always have to do with one's own personhood or with that of another. The goodness or badness of personhood is therefore never only objectively and generally to be established, however much conceptual thinking and its concern for univocal designation is, within its own boundaries, indispensable in this respect.

Conceptual thinking shows its limitations in respect to Being-in-its-totality, which it is never able to comprehend. If it claims universality and totality, Being for it dissolves into the Naught. In the judgment of conceptual thinking Being-in-its-totality is Nothing. So also ethical thinking, if it absolutizes itself in its conceptuality and does not recognize its incompleteness, becomes totally culpable and sees itself delivered over to the unfathomableness of relativity. If in its concern for conceptual clarity ethical thought does not recognize its boundaries, then it would have to admit that what good and evil are can never be established, and further, it would have to ask whether the distinction is valid at all. Actually, an ethical thinking which is not conscious of its boundaries would have to pay for transgressing its boundaries by losing the distinction between good and evil, and sinking into nihilism.

Finally, it can be said that conceptual thinking experiences its boundaries over against the Transcendence out of which we hear the call to responsibility. That this voice is our unconditioned concern cannot be objectively established. A summoning takes place wherever we dare to hear and follow this voice, though we must afterward subject our decision to mature testing and reexamination. If we try to circumvent this risk by codifying the voice of God, we shall have to pay by experiencing deliverance over to an automaton and by becoming automatons ourselves, with the consequence that the freedom of moral responsibility is eliminated.

Therefore, within the whole sphere of personal and corporate existence of Being-in-its-totality and of our relatedness to Transcendence, the criteria of conceptual thinking are to be employed only in the preliminary stages rather than in an authentic, final, and unconditioned way. Statements of such knowledge are always right or wrong. But from this aspect alone they cannot do full justice to their objects. In man, Being, and God, we are not dealing with objects but with things which we grasp in an unconditional way in the awareness of the boundaries of our knowledge and in the actualization of personhood as related to our Transcendence.

To this awareness or actualization of our personhood, we do not apply, therefore, the criteria of right and wrong but, rather, the decision as to what is true or false. A person is not right or wrong. The deeds of a person can be right or wrong, a fact which can be demonstrated within certain limits. But in respect to personhood there is no objective, universally provable rightness or wrongness; rather, there occurs *in it*, i.e., personhood, the truth or the lie. Truth and deception are not to be demonstrated in an objective manner, for truth is something quite different from rightness just as the lie is something quite different from error. We participate in truth or deception whenever we vouch for the truth of which we are persuaded or make a pretense of truth by being irresponsible or pretending responsibility. Truth occurs in our self-actualization as responsible personhood in community. We do not possess truth; rather we can only *be* true. Or we move in the sphere of untruth and deceptions and therefore distort and pervert our personhood. But about ourselves or others we can demonstrate objectively neither the one nor the other. In a final clarity not to be concealed from me, however, I know whether in a specific situation I am true or not. Even a community can occur in which I encounter the other in complete openness and in which he announces his being to me in just such a way.

In any case, truth is always a problem when we violate it. We then become conscious of a split in our being which we attempt to conceal or under whose evidentness we suffer. While we can know exactly with respect to ourselves whether we are in truth or untruth, we cannot establish this with the same immediacy in the case of others—otherwise we would have to become completely one with them. But we can appeal to the truth of the other person and so encounter him as to say, "I expect of you that you do not deceive me, that you do not distort your personhood." Such a distortion happened when Cain became angry with his brother Abel, being jealous over his success in sacrifice. "Then his countenance fell," it says in that passage on fratricide. And with this disfigurement (*Entstellung*), which can also be a disguise (*Verstellung*), he began to be a victim of the power of sin.

In the biblical account the story of Cain is not regarded merely as a human story to be explained psychologically. Rather, it is narrated there in the context of the great history of the acts of God with men. "The acts of God with men," however, is a mythological expression for the unconditionedness of our personhood. If and when I become aware of my unconditioned responsibility, then I have to do with what in the traditional language of faith is designated as God. Untruth, deception, and distortion of personhood are called "sin" in this language. Sin is the distortion of the relatedness to Transcendence through the denial of responsibility. "Am I my brother's keeper?" retorted Cain when God reminded him that the blood of his brother cries up from earth to heaven. Thus he encountered God's curse, to be a fugitive and vagabond. But the one condemned by God also received a secret protective sign by means of which the God who was angry in his hiddenness revealed himself simultaneously as the gracious, reconciling God.

As mythical and magical as this story is, it expresses the view that the recognition of the guilt of sin carries within it the germ of reconciliation. The knowledge of perversion is not itself perverted but contains in itself the possibility of rectifying this perversion. We should not minimize this perversion by some special way of looking at it and reducing it to a merely relative, limited affair. We can avoid the necessity of designating our perverted relation to Transcendence as sin and thus be deprived also of the possibility of restoration, of rectifying this perversion in the realm of persons. Sin is an uncomfortable word. But in its absoluteness it is just that term which alone corresponds to the personal nature of the perversion of our relationship to Transcendence. In the recognition of sin the perverted relationship to Transcendence is again rectified. Recognition of sin is the reconciling sign of Cain, a reconciliation in relationship to Transcendence as well as to humanity. There is reconciliation only for the sinner. In the recognition of sin the possibility of reconciliation hidden within it becomes manifest.

Thus we have distinguished between the realms of right and wrong, true and false, open and hidden, and good and evil. Knowledge, or knowing, is possible only in the first of these, while the other three deal with a being which is manifest only in our self-realization as persons or in the perversion of this personhood. While "right and wrong" is a category of knowledge, the distinctions between true and false, open and hidden, good and evil relate to the realization of our nonobjectifiable personhood in the unconditionedness of its relation to Transcendence. The first category relates to the question "What can we know?"; the last three to the question "What should we do?"

THE NATURE AND INDISPENSABILITY OF ETHICAL NORMS

Despite the characteristic differentiation, however, the knowledge of what is right and the doing of the good cannot be separated. In order to be able to do the good, I have to know what the good is. For the sake of its enactment the good also craves a knowledge of what is right. Without an objectively knowable and applicable criterion the good cannot be separated from evil at all, nor can the good be done and the evil avoided. For responsible actions we need knowable moral norms. The nature of these moral norms, which in their knowable objectivity are useful for the realization of nonobjectifiable personhood, must now be treated.

Basically, it must be said that these norms belong to the world "present at hand." They are present and known objectively in quite different forms and formulations. But they are not content simply to be at hand; rather, they point to something, not which *is* but which *should be*. The norm is certainly something present, but it expresses something which is still to come. What the norm demands can be dismissed, contested, and frustrated. But over against all such rejections, misrepresentations, and disturbances something is still expressed in the norm about that which is to be actualized. The essence of the norm, which demands what should be done, meets us as a whole cosmos of norms in the history of mankind.

Norms grow up out of habit and custom, out of sacred traditions and divine revelations, as well as out of experiences of utility which result from the necessities of human social existence. They are established in specific societal systems and laws of states; they are built up into ethical systems to which are added further great collections of precepts and commentaries. They attain form in definite institutions which support the observance of the norms and punish infractions, in tribal rites, in societal ostracism, in police censure, sanctions of international law, ecclesiastical condemnations, and the threat of divine punishment.

With these historical norms which are constantly changing are associated others of which it may be asserted that they are eternal rather than temporal in origin because they belong to the essence of man. These are the principles of natural law which cannot be violated without penalty—not even by the norms of positive law. If positive law, which achieves its form in custom and society, state and church, violates these eternal principles of natural law, and if there should prove to be aberrations in the foundations of moral norms, appeal is then made to these eternal natural laws and human rights. Thereby it cannot be overlooked that in concrete application natural law constantly needs interpretation, so that in concrete application even its norms assume historical form and can be distinguished from historical and institutional regulations by a special individualism in interpretation.

THE PROBLEMATIC CHARACTER OF ETHICAL NORMS

With this reference to the problematic character of objectively present criteria upon which ethical action is dependent we have already caught sight of the questionable character of all ethical norms. This is apparent not only in the complexity of this realm of norms but also in the fact that individual systems of norms compete with and jeopardize each other. Norms valid at any given time have assumed various forms in the context of different ages and societal regulations.

In order to interpret validly what has become historical, a science can be developed which seeks to predetermine for all possible cases how the norms have to be applied in particular. Such a casuistry, in which all possible cases are seen and decided in advance, is possible in secular and

canon law. But the more univocal such casuistic regulations and applications become, all the more problematic
becomes the nature of the decision between good and evil
insofar as it has to do with personhood. If there is at hand
an authoritatively sanctioned, univocal interpretation of
what is good or evil, then the individual no longer has to
decide. It is already decided for him. He can then only
subject himself to the law which relieves him of responsibility by an objectively demonstrable legalism. This may
happen in a liberal way, or it can lead into oppressive nar-
rowness. In each case, however, personhood is put in jeop-
ardy because personal responsibility has been suspended.
That can be very comfortable—but one's personhood can
be lost in very comfortable ways. It can be sacrificed to an
idol, and in a curious misunderstanding of God this idol
can be either an earthly or heavenly Lawgiver who gave
the laws by which we are bound. There are institutions
which speak so strongly in the name of God that there no
longer remains for the individual any necessity or possibility either of his own discovery of truth or of his own
responsible interpretation by a personal decision. When
truth or deity becomes objective in an institution, subjectivity is permitted only in the sense of total submission,
but that means the abandoning of ethical personhood.
Totalitarianism in a secular or ecclesiastical form always
means the end, the death of personal responsibility. This
threat to personhood can occur even in very human forms.
But it is then all the more dangerous.

THE DANGER OF NIHILISM AND ITS CONQUEST

When we uncover the problematic character of all
norms and the impossibility of ascertaining them objectively, do we not then fall victim to arbitrariness and
autocracy? Do we then have to determine what is good or
evil? This danger of a false subjectivism is not to be disre-

garded and it is no less dangerous than that of the objec-
tivism in which—as we have shown—personal responsibility is sacrificed to a false authority for the sake of a seem-
ingly desirable certainty. It can happen that the person
who revolts against objective forms of authority falls
victim to personal whim and that then our explanation of
the concept of sin is no longer possible: namely, that the
recognition of sin as sin conceals within itself the possibility of rectification.

Falling victim to arbitrariness is a frequent reaction to a
false absolutizing of norms which do not allow room for
personhood and personal relationship to Transcendence.
But even such absolutized norms which endanger personhood do not permit us to overlook the fact that personhood is dependent upon norms and cannot dispense with
them. Resistance to a world of norms which neglects its
historical character should not lead completely to a denial
of the norms and their institutionalized forms. Without
the presence and recognition of ethical norms it is not possible to be or become a person. Without them we would
be delivered over to the Naught which threatens when
we become conscious of the boundaries of what has become historical. Without the existence of norms we would
not be what we have become—we would not be able to
become what we should be. For the Being presented in
the norms is Being that *should be,* the Being that should
become through compliance with the norms. Therefore
the correctly understood norm points beyond the form in
which it is present in traditions and institutions to what-
should-be, which appeals to our personhood. Personhood
matures in orientation to the ever present world of norms
and in debate with them in the responsibility of personal
choice. Thus personhood always moves on a thin line between authority which suppresses personhood, and personal
whim, through which personhood is lost.

In their objective existence criteria are never absolute but always remain relative. They serve to orient us and are subject to revision. The judgment of the conscience, however, is unconditioned and its implementation in my conduct is not subject to revision, insofar as it does not belong merely to the world of objects, but stands in relation to my personhood. I have to make a decision on the basis of criteria which are hereafter recognized as questionable; the decision is my affair and its consequences belong henceforth to my personhood. If I wish to dispense with the fact that decisions pertaining to me belong henceforth to my personhood, I thereby distort the truth of my personhood into a lie. For I slip into untruth if I act as though something which I have decided for myself has not been my decision and has lain outside the sphere of my responsibility.

The origin of nihilism does not lie in the relativizing of ethical criteria but in the wish to be irresponsible which appeals unjustly to the relativity of these criteria. Nihilism is the consequence of that unbelief which is the escape from the acceptance of unconditional responsibility. But the overcoming of nihilism is possible where we are ready unconditionally to take on the responsibility for decisions which have occurred and will occur in the realm of relativity, and, therefore, to speak not merely of mistakes and tragedy, but of sin and personal guilt as well. And we must do this in spite of the relativity of all ethical norms, a relativity not to be denied but recognized for the sake of our personhood.

Without advancing into the realm of faith it is not possible to speak appropriately about good and evil. Whoever knows about sin and guilt also knows about reconciliation and grace. Without reconciliation and grace goodness is not possible; but *through them* evil is to be overcome.

6

History and Faith

In everything said previously we have not only continually encountered history but have become conscious of ourselves as standing within history as well.

THE CATEGORIES FOR DEALING WITH HISTORY

Even as we dealt with the nature of cognition, with its way and what is to be reached on it, we were not in a position to present a completed, unified system by means of which we could gain possession of the truth once and for all. The assertion of such a system would not take into account our historicality, or historical dimension. In history there are only relative exactitudes, and only within this relativity can the truth in which we personally participate dawn upon us in an unqualified way. This practical truth is not a position which we can occupy but a way upon which we encounter other positions and upon which there is a constant passing from decision to decision. Knowing takes place in history and shows abundant traces of it; even when we wish to become clear about this situation of knowledge in which we find ourselves we are stamped by the past and by the knowledge which we have from it. When we begin to think we find ourselves already in history. We would not be what we are without tradition, without the living language in which the knowledge of the past is given to us. Only by taking over this heritage are we able to determine our vantage point and its modifications. We live by values which are transmitted to us. They enable us to test and decide. In every connection we see ourselves in history as stamped by history. We can distance ourselves from it but we still experience it as that which determines us in our innermost nature, so that we never really stand over against it but rather form a part of this history.

In the second place, man is not merely a part of history; rather, history really deals with man. Our second theme is this: man is simultaneously the theme of history. There are, to be sure, events and courses of events which stand in some kind of relation to each other. But they would not constitute history without man, to whom the history pertains, who experiences himself as embedded in this event, but who also stands over against it and forms it, seeks its meaning and gives information about it. Nature is certainly full of appearances of meanings, but it is in fact man who establishes these relationships and the meaningfulness of natural events. Nature knows neither about its meaninglessness nor its meaning; rather, it is man who conceives history under these aspects. It is true that man himself is an object of this event—for example, of a natural catastrophe. But a natural catastrophe as a mere occurrence is no historical event. Only if such a natural occurrence involves persons, as was the case with the Basel earthquake of 1356, and only if man can say of it, "We were saved by the skin of our teeth," so that we have information as to how this event affected lives, the life of a state or of a people, and caused this state or this people to begin anew and to frame history—only then does a natural occurrence become an historical event. That only happens where man plays a role—as one affected by the occurrence and also as one who tells about it, who seeks the meaning of such an occurrence, and who also constructively intervenes and attempts to realize something meaningful. The powers of nature are utilized by man; he controls nature and uses its powers as presuppositions of human life in his development of culture and technology. Man is not only the one who seeks meaning but the one who also creates it. He can experience himself as lost in the immense cosmos—but he is still the one who knows of his own magnitude, and still the one who knows that, as Sophocles says, there is nothing greater than man. The cosmos would not be what it is—speaking externally—without the man who disappears in the cosmos. It is man alone who constitutes the world into a cosmos, a cosmos of history.

In this way a third characteristic of history becomes evident, namely, that wherever man has proved himself to be that one apart from whom history would not be history because it is an event at whose center he stands both questioning and shaping, both being oppressed and pressing forward—there man also experiences his absolute boundary which cannot be crossed. He experiences himself as "thrown" into this event, whose origin he can seek but never really know because it is an event of whose ultimate source and destiny he does not have knowledge, an event in which he fancies himself only as a wave in a stream which emerges and again disappears. But he is no mere wave because he is conscious of this wave-like character of his existence, even though he is "thrown" into this river whose origin and end he cannot conceptualize. In that case do its beginning in time and its end really belong to history? What is the meaning of eternity? Is there really a bridge from time into this other sphere about which we have some information from history, though in the special form of myths, of stories about the gods?

Are these stories to be considered part of what we designate as history, namely, that realm at whose center man stands? Historical science establishes the existence of such stories. And while it can recognize an historical core in the sagas—even though this is surrounded by fantastic ideas—no such claim can be made for events described in the myths. The mythical world appears to history as the mere scenery of human history. Historical science is not able to know what stands behind them or is delineated by them. Myth forms the boundary or limit of history. But what here is really the *limiter* and what the *limited*? Is the meaning of myth such that it can express something about the meaning of history?

Fourth: It belongs to the nature of history that man has to ask what role he should play in history and what relationship he should sustain to the norms which are transmitted to him in history and which wish to give an answer to the question of good and evil. What appears as normative in the different forms is that which distinguishes history from nature. The responsibility of which we become aware through ethical norms elevates us out of nature. But it is precisely history itself which discloses the relativity of traditional norms. In that way it cancels itself out. The man who states that history proves everything is relative and that nothing is eternally valid is probably correct from a purely historical point of view; but in this way he not only frees himself from false absolutizing, but extinguishes himself as a person and sinks into a stream which is no longer history but a mere natural occurrence. This, however, is no longer the occurrence at whose center stands the man who seeks meaning and who knows himself to be responsible for meaningful behavior.

In the fifth and final place, there belongs to the nature of history the question which we have now met in different forms: What is the real meaning of the curious, discordant totality of this occurrence which we call history? Does it have an ultimate meaning or does it present an ultimately insoluble riddle?

THE NATURE OF HISTORY IN HISTORICAL SCIENCE, HISTORICAL ACT, AND THE INTERPRETATION OF HISTORY

If we summarize what we have already encountered in all our previous considerations as the nature of history which is never finally conceivable but is nevertheless so immediately our concern, then we can say: History presents a sequence of occurrences about which we can gain information and which we can investigate, but it is never merely this knowable past. In our understanding of history we are, rather, continually determined and stamped by history itself. We are, however, not simply delivered over to it but we participate in it actively and creatively so that we are responsible for its future. Without the participation of man in this sequence of occurrences the sequence would not constitute history. Nevertheless it is not simply a human product. Man experiences himself as "thrown" into history and in it he experiences his boundaries in such a way that he has to inquire after the goal and origin, the essence and meaning of this occurrence. He is not, however, able to answer this question objectively and with universal validity.

Does the enigmatical character of this phenomenon lie in the fact that—as has been the case already in this characterization—history can be discussed under three quite different perspectives? First: history as something which can be investigated, which is an object of research, of historical science. Second: history which men constitute as historical personalities, as generals, as politicians, as great spirits of the world who make their mark on an epoch. Third: history is made, it occurs. But what it is becomes apparent only in the way it is interpreted in historical research and historical enactment. Therefore, to investigate history, to make history, to interpret history—these involve three quite different notions of history. Each commends itself to someone as something special. We would now like to present the three different possibilities for an understanding of history which result from this classification.

First: History can be investigated with the aid of historical science. This science provides access to documents of all kinds from which we are able to learn what has happened earlier. In order for this to be achieved, the extant sources must be tested for their historical reliability and correctness. We still do not know what really happened simply from the fact that an occurrence is documented. Records can be—consciously or unconsciously—very subjectively colored, just as they can be—also consciously or unconsciously—interpreted in a highly subjective way. Is an objective knowledge of the past possible at all? Perhaps—in certain external sequences and facts, names and dates. But even with such an exact reconstruction of what has occurred or once has been, the essence of history is still not grasped. History is something more than what can be dated and cataloged. History is not merely a source for museum collections of an object of science, though both certainly belong to history. In these contexts history, as a rule, seldom occurs.

History occurs where history is made. That can happen in history (*Historie*), for example, so that the opposite of what has held as historical up to that time is proclaimed and an attempt is made to actualize a new program of history through political or military operations. In this way an entire culture with its archives and museums can be destroyed and a new era of history can then be explained in new history books and a new concept of history can be advanced which must be held as the true view of past and present. History is then the *fable convenue* which the victor creates.

As much as we loath such totalitarian history because of its deceptions and violence, it must be admitted that in all real understanding of history something of such "fabrication" plays a role—only not in terms of the brutality which is so vivid in our minds. Because man is an historical being, determined and summoned by history, he cannot stand over against history at an objective distance. Without personal participation in history he does not really deal with history at all and is not able to understand it in its nature. We cannot and should not stand over against history in detached objectivity; we must rather interpret it responsibly from our personal participation in it.

Such interpreting of history is more than a mere ascertaining of what has been. It is also something quite different from an arbitrary, dictatorial fabrication of history. It is a personal participation in the event, participation which presupposes research and the most objective orientation possible, but is not thereby allowed to rest. Even this objectivity is not possible without the inclusion of our subjectivity because history—as opposed to a merely natural occurrence—has to do with the subjectivity of man. But a genuine understanding of history is not made complete when an historical picture is obtained from the perspective of our subjectivity. The knowledge of the necessary subjectivity of our picture of history entails for us an obligation, namely, the obligation to assume our responsibility in history. We neither have the knowledge of the World-Mind about the meaning of history, nor are we simply delivered over to historical fate; rather, we are required to exhibit the truth of our interpretation of history by the way in which we assume responsibility for the interpretation of our situation, and subsequently by the way in which from this responsibility we grasp the possibilities for the future construction of history. The interpretation of history is a matter of faith which involves unconditioned responsibility.

THE HISTORY OF THE INTERPRETATIONS OF HISTORY

As different as these faith-interpretations of history are from history itself, it is clear that they also belong to history (*Historie*). They are themselves objects of historical research and they continue in a succession of ever new interpretations to live in a history which gives us opportunity to clarify our own interpretations of our historical existence. From the beginnings of our history they have emerged in the form of myths concerning the beginning of all things, depicting an event in which man does not play the primary role but in which cosmic powers, day and night, heaven and earth, rule; Chaos is overcome; gods are born, and generations of the gods struggle with one another. In these struggles the world is created by the gods, and men and peoples understand themselves as offspring of the gods. From this starting point the myths peer into the future and tell how everything will come to an end in a downfall or consummation and how everything will then begin all over again. Such, at any rate, is what is transmitted to us by Hesiod about the Greeks.

In Greek philosophy the gods were superseded by principles of being. These principles rule and constitute the world in a universal process the origin and end of which cannot be conceived and which forms a unified Being. Individual thinkers, however, foresaw within the world-process a recurring downfall of the existing world by conflagration and subsequent emergence of a new world. For such a view of the world and of history—a view which presupposes an eternal cycle, a dissolution of individual worlds within an all-encompassing totality which has neither beginning nor end—the enigmatic question of the beginning of history is dismissed. Being was always there, encompassing the beginning as well as the end, and of this the myths contain the story. For thinking, however, there is only an eternal Being into which man is "thrown" and

79

with whose laws he has to comply. If he rebels against them he is punished by the gods for his *hybris*.

We meet a quite different concept of history in the Bible, although even there one finds the initial record of the overcoming of an existing Chaos. That Chaos which is overcome by God is the primeval dragon of the Babylonian myth of creation. But this cosmic drama is employed in the Old Testament as an expression of the historical consciousness of the people of Israel. What had been described in the original myth as the overcoming of the dragon was experienced by Israel in its release from Egypt and in all its other conquests over its enemies which had occurred in the course of its history. When in its worship it praised God as creator it did so not only in grateful remembrance of previous historical experiences but also in the confidence and hope that God would in the future also crush its enemies and give his people the victory over the dragons which threatened them. When at a later time Israel saw itself delivered over to the powers of world history in an event which dissolved the nation, then the original cosmic form of this historical myth changed in such a way that salvation came to be expected as a new creation which God would allow to intervene through his Messiah. In the New Testament the messianic hope is heightened to an expectation of an imminent end of the world and the advent of a new aeon. In this end-event the "old serpent" is finally overcome and the kingdom of God breaks in upon the earth.

The Christian church and its eschatological hope grew out of this apocalyptic form of the biblical hope and the delay of its fulfillment. This hope affirms that Jesus will, as he promised, return as the Messiah. Even though the expected return is delayed and history temporarily continues on there is still in history the community of those who expect this Messiah. To the degree that the world continues to exist, the church directs itself to this world, with the result that in its subsequent understanding of history it also positively incorporates the existence of this world. The *civitas terrena*, the secular city, is encircled by the super-earthly history, the *civitas Dei*, the heavenly city which will finally gain the victory. Although even in the biblical-Christian view there is talk of periods which supersede one another, periods which are symbolized by different metals, as in the Graeco-Roman period, there is no endless change; it is not Being but God who is alone eternal. But does not the eternal fall victim to time when it is expressed in time?

Thus it is understandable that in modern scientific views of history the question as to the beginning and end of Being recedes, though Being itself is seen in an immanent development directed toward a goal. In this way modern evolutionism combines the ancient thinking about Being and the biblical-Christian thinking about history. But the problems of the Greek notion of Being and of the biblical-Christian mythology of history are solved neither by abandoning the question of an absolute beginning and end of history nor by replacing the supernatural-divine guidance of history with the idea of immanent progress. These problems rather reemerge in new forms within this modern picture of history. For the science which knows neither creation at the beginning nor the kingdom of God as a goal, Being becomes the Naught and hope for the future melts into utopia. In view of the unfathomable depths which have yawned before us in the human soul and in the possibilities of technology, is it surprising that bourgeois optimism has today given way to a nihilistic existentialism which in the daring defiance with which it attempts to encounter its destiny is more like Sisyphus than Prometheus? But as the other by-product of idealism, does not dialectical materialism constitute a chimera when it hopes that through the messianism of the proletariat a paradise of humanity will emerge out of the Chaos? It is curious how precisely in the so-called scientific-philosophical views of history the slain myths and long-rejected speculations continue to live on. Views of history—like views of the world—cannot claim to be a critical science conscious of its boundaries; rather, they necessarily assume mythological-speculative forms. Precisely in this fact do they attain their character as expressions of human self-understanding, that is, as expressions of a faith which in its nature is specifically dependent upon myths and speculative formulations for the appropriate forms of its expression.

THE DECEPTION OF THE PICTURES OF HISTORY AND THE RISK OF OUR HISTORICALITY

These pictures of history become deceptive at the moment in which their representatives are no longer clear about the ways in which they speak and about the spheres in which they encounter each other. From testimonies of faith ideologies emerge which make the claim of universally-valid scientific truth. While testimonies of faith prove their genuineness by being conscious that their special insight into truth cannot be generalized and cannot be made compulsory, ideologies—on the other hand—do not know these boundaries for the expression and utilization of our knowledge of history but wish in order to gain power to control the individual and the political community in some kind of absolute system. But what emerges in history as faith is never protected against such a perversion of its nature and its truth. Ideologies are constantly borne along by a faith, albeit, a faith which misunderstands itself, a superstition. A speculative mind can be tempted to interpret mythologically even this strange, but nevertheless dreadful, masquerade of ideological powers—whether or not it believes in progress. But even such an interpretation of history would not avoid the judgment of history, which permits no person to go unpunished for any disregard of his historicality. This is true for any interpretation of history (including that of the traditional Christian faith), however it may be qualified.

What follows for us from the history of the interpretations of history which we depicted in bold strokes from its mythical beginnings to the present time? One thing which results is the admission that we are not in a position to trace a unified, valid historical perspective. The pictures which intrude upon us jeopardize each other precisely because of their manifold variety and opposition. Every assertion of an exclusive view oversteps the boundaries of our knowledge and makes us blind to the risk of our historicality—and also to its opportunity.

The risk consists in the fact that we must dare to make decisions about our conduct and place in history without a total perspective. We cannot get along without some view of history. The only question is whether we use it like a house in which we regard ourselves as secure, or whether we are conscious that it is only a possibility for orienting ourselves, a possibility about which it must be said, "We have here no abiding city, for we await the one which is to come."

But precisely in this open-endedness and in this lack of certainty about our possibility of being oriented lies the special opportunity of our historicality. Responsibility as it belongs to personhood would not be possible at all other than as based on the presupposition of this ultimate openness in which nothing and no one can assume the responsibility for our decisions. In such personhood there is to be found not only the presupposition for understanding history; it constitutes, much more, the nature of that which gives to us in such understanding the very meaning of this phenomenon. The nature and meaning of history are actualized simultaneously and at once wherever men both know themselves in community to be unconditionally responsible, and constitute the sphere of their personal and corporate existence from this understanding of self and of others. Just as becoming a person is a personal matter and not an impersonal possession and continually affords an immediate beginning in unconditionality, so it also occurs only in community and in the context of an understanding within whose possibilities we always see ourselves and by which we are stamped and conditioned. We are each of us already in history when we understand history. But in this understanding of our historicality we are each responsible for what history is. History, like personhood, is never merely something given but a task still to be actualized.

The pictures of historical interpretations which are traditional with us, with which we engage in debate, which we either denounce or appropriate, transform or replace—these pictures are not history itself, however much they may belong to history. They are trail marks along the paths which have been or are to be trod and by which we orient ourselves. And they point further along to that which stands before us as a task in our present situation. They point to the future which is still to be realized, whose meaning is disclosed to us to the degree that we march into it responsibly.

THE MEANING OF THE HOUR

In conclusion, we wish to clarify this with a picture, which is, however, more than a picture. Do we not frequently hear the tolling of the bells when we awaken in the morning? In my home I hear them ring from the Church of St. Martin, followed by those of the Cathedral, together with those of St. Theodore's across the Rhine. By counting I try to separate the strokes and know that it has

84

struck so many times, thus it is six or seven
o'clock. ... But is that the hour which has now struck? Is
there only this time which we measure? Is there not also a
completely different time which can occur at the same
moment as that where the hands on the clock point? Even
at this very moment on the other side of the globe men
can be occupied with the same problems, can experience
fortune or misfortune just as we. The time which our
clocks indicate passes like a natural occurrence. But in this
elapsed time we become conscious that we too have grown
older and that there are possibilities offered to us in it. A
day awaits us with its tasks. We grasp the meaning of time
by doing that which should be done in this hour. History
occurs there where we—orienting ourselves to measurable
time—go to work, sieze the opportunities which the day
affords and attempt to actualize them.

Such unpretentious experience and behavior have more
to do with history than much discourse about history. But
as we understand the great interpretations of history only
from within the actualization of our own historicality, so
they assist us in interpreting the significance of the hour
which wishes to break in upon us, as happens in the Morning Song of a contemporary poet:

> The gloomy nights give way to days,
> The sun extends its glorious rays
> And lets us live in joy.
> Now we would try in this new day
> All the things it brings our way
> To cherish and enjoy.
>
> In this our world God gives Himself
> To us, and would above all else,
> A hymn of praise be sung.
> This is, O Man, of life the sense
> That you the gift should recompense—
> An act of love unsung.[1]

---

[1] Arno Pötzsch, *Gesangbuch der evangelisch-reformierten Kirche der
deutschsprachigen Schweiz* ("Hymnal of the Evangelical Reformed Church
of German-Speaking Switzerland"), No. 81.

7

Thinking Faith as Christian Faith

Up to this point we have indicated at a half-dozen places what thinking faith could be—in respect to cognition, man, Being, God, good and evil, and the question of the meaning of history. In all of this we have struck upon questions and positions of the Christian faith. In the question of cognition, the problem of reason and revelation; in anthropology, the concept of the image of God; in ontology, the question of creation; in metaphysics, faith in God; in ethics, the commandment of God; and in philosophy of history, the hope in the kingdom of God. In the history of Christianity thinking and faith have been indissolubly intertwined. To be sure, philosophy is older than Christianity; but philosophy as we know it is unthinkable apart from Christianity—not only in the past but in the future as well. Even though Western cultural history to the present day has been full of debates between thinking and faith, Christian faith cannot exist apart from thinking. It can even signify an advancement and deepening of philosophical thinking. Certainly there are forms of Christian faith which will have nothing to do with thinking as presented here—and they make the sign of the cross before such presentations as if before the Devil. But such so-called faith would suffer no harm by exposing itself to the criticism of thinking and by learning that it could be purified and deepened in this way. That would, however, signify a risk, and many seek no risk in faith and wish not to expose their faith to transformation. They prefer their familiar faith to a thinking faith, not realizing that thinking faith is Christian faith, and that today true Christian faith can be only thinking faith.

It is precisely this point, that thinking faith is for us at the same time Christian faith, which we wish to elaborate in connection with the points just mentioned. This gives us the opportunity simultaneously to survey once again the whole of the completed course.

FAITH IN THE MOVEMENT OF THOUGHT

First: There are indeed views of the Christian faith that are unacceptable to philosophical thinking or that can be brought into relation with it only in ways which are complicated and because they are deceptive, ultimately untenable. There are forms of the Christian faith which, though essentially incompatible with philosophical thinking, seek concord with it, and there seem to be some types of philosophy which can ally with such faith. There are conceptions of faith, such as the acceptance of specific statements on the grounds of supernatural authorities like the Bible or the church, which arrest thinking and demand of it that for the sake of its own salvation it subordinate itself "in praiseworthy fashion," as the church so beautifully puts it. Where thinking comes into conflict with what this faith represents as divine truth, it has to subject itself to the dogma of the church or to the "It is written"; and if thinking is not prepared to do this, it is rejected as heretical.

Genuine thinking will not be prepared for such a *sacrificium intellectus* but gladly accepts its condemnation for the sake of truth. A concession becomes less difficult when the ecclesiastical institutions and judges of faith are not as absolute and infallible as they customarily behave. How many decisions of the church with respect to doctrine and judgments about faith have not already been revised in the course of history! There is in addition to the history of thinking a history of faith—and it has not always been retrogressive. Moreover, the changes have constantly been made with the aid of thinking—to be sure, of a mistreated thinking when the thinking was deposed or deprecated by faith. In this case thinking has been required to inquire of itself whether in its knowledge it has not actually gone astray. It has as little right to absolutize itself as have the institutions of Christian faith which it encounters. It faces the constant danger of overstepping its boundaries. There is every reason for faith to inquire of such thinking whether it knows of its boundaries or whether it regards itself as thoroughly competent to say what is the case with man and the world, and what God, good and evil, and the meaning of history are. Thinking can become as dogmatic or even more dogmatic than what it denounces. If for the sake of their common interests they wish to renounce all absolutizations on both sides and become conscious of their boundaries, then thinking and Christian faith can truly encounter each other and find themselves. Such a real encounter can be aided by the consideration that we do not have to do simply with thinking or with Christian faith but always with historical formulations of thinking and Christian faith. Out of such an encounter of thinking and Christian faith something new could emerge, namely, a Christian faith which would be simultaneously a truly thinking faith.

Thinking faith signifies an openness and willingness to be subjected to inquiry, and, at the same time, a coming-to-itself and a decision. On the one hand, it is valid to recognize and take into account the preliminary character of our insights. On the other, one cannot always remain only in suspense but must take a risk with his present insights, however preliminary. The more substantial and

significant the objects with which it deals, the more important is our decision, and all the more significant the choice
for which we must accept the responsibility. Precisely in
matters of faith are there decisions for which no objective
demonstrations of correctness are possible because the concern is with truth which can be demonstrated only in the
open act of concerned involvement. Accordingly we do
not simply have to take over the traditions of our own or
alien faiths; rather, we have to consider whether and how
in our own responsibility we may appropriate them to
ourselves—not as completed possessions of knowledge but
as expressions of our faith which are supported by these
traditions. and which can be grasped only in enactment.
How could thinking not make room for such a faith which
is enacted in a knowledge which remains open-ended and
in unconditioned responsibility? And what could be more
advantageous for the traditional forms of faith than to
enter into and belong to the vital concerns of a thinking
faith? Faith does not absolve us from responsibility but
places us in responsibility. Such faith belongs to the
nature of man.

THE MAN OF FAITH

Now we come to the second point at which thinking
faith has to demonstrate its genuine Christian character,
i.e., to the question of the nature of man. Scientific-
philosophical anthropology and Christian faith make similar objective pronouncements about man. In the Bible
man is regarded as the crown of creation. At the same time
he appears as a lost sinner. But he can be redeemed from
this fallenness through Christ. In what they say about
man, philosophy and science present a similar triad. There
are anthropologists who regard man as the peak of
organic and mental development, the highest creature of
evolution, while for others man represents only a vanish-

ing point in infinity, without significance for cosmic occurrence and—measured by his life—something decadent and
unqualified for life. But simultaneously there is knowledge of the possibility that man, however he may now be
regarded—whether as the highest creature of the development or as decadence of life—understands himself to be
definitely something other than a betrayer of life, namely,
a Superman. In both cases man is not simply identified
with his present imperfect or detestable nature. He is the
"still unfinished animal." He can still attain and actualize
himself. Of all beings he exhibits himself as that one
which possesses the capacity to decide how he shall understand himself and, through the way in which he understands himself, to determine what he shall be.

This insight which we encounter in modern philosophy
and science does not contradict the claim of the Christian
faith that man is created by God for freedom, a freedom
not to be possessed but actualized. The biblical-Christian
concept that man is created by God for the realization of
his freedom corresponds rather well to the anthropological
thesis about the nature of man as a creature who is not
completed but has to decide about his nature. In this way
even the investigator and thinker can know about creature-
liness, for he discovers himself within the situation designated by that anthropological thesis. He can experience
it as a "being condemned to freedom." He has not
invented this determination to freedom but rather experiences it frequently enough as an appointed destiny, which
failure to grasp would mean the loss of his genuine opportunity. As the grasping of his appointed destiny and its
realization in self-understanding signifies the fulfillment of
a being called to personhood, so its lack is experienced as a
failure and sense of guilt. Knowledge of our responsibility
excludes mere discourse about fallenness. As failure means
judgment, so attainment means grace. He who, because of

the way he understands himself, stands guilty before the loss of his destiny can no more withdraw into a consciousness of tragedy than the one to whom success is given has reason for pride. No good achievement can become an occasion of *hybris* for him; on the contrary, it becomes a grateful awareness of having been spared. Or positively expressed, a grateful awareness of experienced grace.

This character of the givenness of all achievement in the actualization of our destiny to responsible personhood is precisely what is meant in the New Testament message of Christ the Redeemer. Christ calls man to his responsibility before God and enables him to assume this responsibility. Therefore he speaks of sin and is aware of the way to reconciliation. It is the way of an about-face which leads to a New Being. Its achievement is grace. The Apostle Paul describes this event as a being transformed in Christ who is the image of God. This event, however, is not bound up with either Jesus or the mythology of the Christ. It occurs wherever man understands himself as absolutely responsible and experiences the fulfillment of his destiny. However powerful historically the Christian ideas and concepts have become for this redeeming self-understanding, its content is not bound to these historical forms. However much they may serve to mediate its truth, they have also to the same degree obstructed it. That happened and happens principally wherever the unconditionality of the grace of personhood is mistaken for historical uniqueness. Why should it be that only Christianity should know about the genuine nature of man as a person summoned to grace? Where but in the New Testament itself is Christ designated as the Logos of creation?

CREATION IN CHRIST

Third: What does creation mean? For the Christian faith God created the world at the beginning out of nothing and he sustains it by his continuing creative power which is bound to no law but is to be regarded as a miracle. This traditional form of the Christian belief in creation was criticized by science principally on the ground of the age of the earth and the origin of life. In association with philosophy it also denied the idea of creation because neither a creation out of nothing nor a beginning of the world is conceivable, and therefore it prefers to speak of the eternity of the world. Furthermore, natural sciences and in their ways historical sciences have discovered universal interrelations of cause and effect which permit no supernatural factors. The stopgap role which is occasionally reserved for God in such systems, usually for apologetic reasons, attests neither to a scientific conclusion nor to an especially deep piety.

Taking such positions is on either side scarcely tenable today. Serious representatives of the Christian faith have no intention of playing the biblical story of creation off against science and its findings or of arguing with the Bible against science. Genuine piety is aware that the explanation of miracles is always an impious thing, whether on apparently natural or supernatural grounds. All proof is inappropriate to miracle. But even modern science and philosophy are today newly conscious of their boundaries with respect to the world and its origin. The natural sciences speak of infinite times and spaces, but they nevertheless reckon with the possibility of a beginning and a finitude of the world within a world-picture which is certainly intangible and only to be conceived mathematically. Use is also made of such models as that of "curved space." In light of the most spiritualized formations of a physical world-view, philosophy is also conscious that a world-picture as such is an impossibility insofar as it attempts to mediate a picture of the world in its totality. Philosophy claims that only individual aspects of the world are accessible to us because we belong to the world and that as historical creatures.

The change within science and philosophy indicated above in no way means that room is created for the biblical mythology in the sense that it is to be given priority over or simply attached to self-limiting natural science as a kind of super-science or super-philosophy. In any event faith does better when it concedes to science that which belongs to science and sets up no mythological hypotheses within what is to be explained scientifically. The world-pictures of modern physics are fantastic enough to compensate the human soul hungering after curiosities. The philosophical dissolution of world-pictures makes room for faith by indicating what lies behind the problematical and inescapable tendency of thinking toward world-pictures, namely, that man is in need of such portrayals of Being for his own self-understanding. We belong to the world, and in order to comprehend ourselves in our nature as conditioned by space and time we have to put our thinking about ourselves into space and time. Space and time form the locale for the realization of our destiny.

The world is the realm of our self-actualization because we in our nature are not world-less—that is also what is meant in the biblical account of creation when *dominium terrae,* lordship over the earth, is assigned to man. The same is the meaning of the New Testament when it speaks of the sighing creature who awaits the revelation of the sons of God in order to fulfill his destiny through space and time and through that which is in space and time.

We experience what creation is, the unconditioned beginning and the event which leads back to none other than the mystery of the creative word, when we become aware of having been summoned to responsible person-hood. Personhood means to know in all relativity that one is unconditionally responsible. In every responsible thought and act an absolute beginning takes place. From the perspective of objective knowledge, what preceded man and what proceeds from him belongs in the realm of what is causally conditioned, a realm which seems to be without beginning and end. On this level creation is unthinkable, save as we understand it as the realm of the actualization of our responsible personhood. Creation is not a matter for knowledge but takes place for faith. It occurs—when we think about what the Apostle Paul said about faith as "being in Christ"—in Christ. Thus it is not surprising that the Gospel of John identifies the creative word in the first chapter of the Bible with the Logos appearing in Christ. This mythological speculation is simply a statement of the self-understanding of responsible personhood and of the understanding of the world bound up with it. It is thinking faith's understanding of creation.

THE GOD WHO MAKES US RESPONSIBLE

Fourth: For such a faith God is neither a mere mythology to be regarded as true nor a First Cause to be proven from the world. It is superstitious to affirm that the existence of God is to be held as true because faith demands it or that he can be proven because there must be a First Cause. There are forms of the Christian faith which consist in large measure of nothing more than such half-mythological, half-scientific superstition. The case is much different with the God of thinking faith. He is experienced as reality in the history of the individual and the community in which man experiences himself as summoned to the realization of his humanity and co-humanity. This summons is neither simply to be maintained as true, nor theoretically to be proven; it rather occurs in every situation in which our responsibility comes to consciousness. God is the power who summons us to responsibility and gives us the possibility for its actualization.

But we are confronted with failure where we do not hear the call and do not perceive the grace. Here a reality is dealt with which is present with the awareness of our humanity in the world and in history. We have created neither our being nor our responsibility, but discover that we are predetermined for it. But even then we can pervert this being and experience the loss of our destiny as judgment. The God who is the concern of the thinking awareness of responsible life is neither a First Cause to be proven and therefore contested nor merely a mystery before which we can only be silent and into which we sink. For our personhood God himself is personal in the voice which summons us to responsibility. He is not identical with the picture which we make of him by analogy with our personhood when we speak of his word, his speaking, his presence, his judgment, his grace, and his mercy. But these pictures do correspond to the reality of which we become aware in the act of coming to ourselves as persons. We would have to deny our personhood if we wished not to recognize this truth.

The truth of such faith in God occurs in responsible relationship, that is, in prayer to God and in service to man. For both types of the responsible relationship to Transcendence—the service of God and the service of man—we have to discover for ourselves the true forms and opportunities. But in one as in the other we are dependent upon traditional possibilities. We are impoverished in prayer if we are not at home with a specific manner of worshiping God, in which our soul is at ease, and if we are not familiar with the great liturgy which is permeated with the poetry, art, and religions of all times. Furthermore, even in service to man—without which service to God would be an idle business—we are dependent upon the structures of corporate human life in which we find ourselves in past and present.

95

GOD'S COMMANDMENT IN ETHICS

God and men always encounter us already preformed. Without these formations we could speak neither with God nor men. We are dependent upon language which we have not invented. But that does not absolve us from responsibility for that which is valid in it. This leads us to the fifth thing to be said about thinking and Christian faith: Responsibility, as introduced above, presupposes knowledge of good and evil. Responsibility requires for its enactment a criterion for the choice of possibilities, for their recognition and their realization. This is as equally true for philosophy as it is for Christian faith. Christian faith utilizes for this purpose the commandments of God over against which man appears as sinner. This happens in such a way that man is thereby drawn into a divine salvation event through which he is justified before God and enabled to fulfill the commandments. For philosophy there is no such commandment of God. It takes cognizance of the emergence of pronouncements which go back to divine oracles and arise with divine authority. However, it does not simply acknowledge them; it rather establishes their historical relativity. It sees them on a par with other criteria of value to which it seeks to orient itself. In any case, it deems the acknowledgment of values indispensable for the realization of humanity. These values can be derived from the realms of nature or of the spirit in which realms the presupposition for their realization is seen. They are actualized by man or, despite his behavior, impregnated with a world law that fulfills itself one way or another, either by including man or passing him by.

In the history of both philosophy and the Christian faith different ethics and correspondingly different conceptions of culture stand opposed to each other. But even then their mutual interactions are not to be overlooked.

Occasionally, philosophical ethics has influenced Christian faith, and conversely Christian faith has determined philosophical ethics, even though all of the ideas of the former were not thereby accepted. Even within the Bible, however, there are great differences and modifications as to what God demands and commands. One has only to think of the different attitudes toward enemies or toward cultic commandments in the Old and New Testaments.

But despite all the mutual interaction, modifications, common characteristics, and opposites which have permeated the whole history of the interchange between philosophy and the Christian faith, they are both beset at three points by a problem not only having to do with their history, but of essential importance to us as well. In the Christian faith the three critical elements are called commandment, sin, and reconciliation. These correspond to the moral good, evil, and the overcoming of evil in philosophical ethics. Without a serious regard for the philosophical problems one cannot speak of commandment, sin, and reconciliation in the sense of a thinking Christian faith. And only in the context of such a faith is it possible to deal adequately with the meaning of good, evil, and the overcoming of evil.

First: God's commandment is the commandment of God because it is given by God—irrespective of what man may say from the perspective of his ethical judgment. God's commandment is not to be criticized by man since then it would not be God's command. But at what place is God's commandment to be known? When man decides this he no longer confronts God's command but becomes the lawgiver. But if God's commandment were to be known apart from our taking a position, then the decision would be taken from us and we would no longer be responsible in a genuine sense.

Thus, sin is the failure to acknowledge God's commandment. Before God evil is sin. But the evaluation of evil as sin is God's prerogative alone. For this reason the philosopher avoids the term sin and speaks of evil as the worthless, the opposite of the good. But does he not pretend to deity if he thinks that he possesses an absolute criterion for deciding between good and evil?

And finally, the idea of the possibility of an overcoming of sin or evil appears problematical. Is sin really taken seriously if it is regarded as surmountable? Can it be transmitted and washed away by baptism? Or can Christ vicariously assume the guilt of our sins? Is the guilt which is a part of our responsible personhood transferable to another like a debt? The material consequences of personal guilt can be taken over by another—but not the guilt itself. On the other hand, philosophical ethical theories are fraught with illusions about the improvement of the human race and offer dubious means for the so-called betterment of the world.

At any rate, both Christian faith and philosophical thought have sufficient reason in all three instances not to become rigid in systems but to recognize their problems and to remain open to each other.

What could result as the ethical perspective of a thinking faith is just this: that God's commandment is different from an ethical norm. While an ethical norm can be grounded and proven, God's command as such is beyond proof. After all, when we orient ourselves to ethical norms, is it not the case that when we wish to come to a decision and deed we have to suspend our testing and reflecting, measuring and weighing, and that in the whole relativity from which we are not able to escape we experience unconditionality when we take the risk with our enduringly preliminary insights? God's commandments are known to us only as ethical norms and we have to test such ethical norms. Unconditionality, as it belongs essentially to God's command, occurs whenever we—on the basis of the insight given to us—take an unconditional risk as God's command requires. In and with our unconditional and hazardous willingness to obey, the norm becomes for us God's command, but not in such a way that we put God's command at our disposal in the form of a norm and thus know once and for all what God's command is. In that case we would have exchanged God's command for a falsely absolutized norm and would thus have to do neither with a valid norm nor with God's command. God's command is perceived only in the act of unconditioned decision and it cannot be proven outside this act. But what we hear in each of these acts as the voice of God depends upon how we test it outside that nonobjectifiable and unconditioned act in the context of the objective world of ethical norms. Unconditionality and conscientiousness belong together and cannot replace each other. Without deceiving others and, above all, ourselves, we can hear God not only by taking seriously our own insights but by remaining ready to assume the consequences of a faulty hearing, remaining open to corrections which result from a new reflection and hearing and using the time at our disposal for the expiation of the perverted and the realization of the right.

THE REAL SALVATION HISTORY

In this way we find ourselves surrounded by the reality which is proclaimed in the Christian faith as God's salvation history. For thinking faith, the view of history in the scheme of creation, sin, reconciliation through Christ, and eschatological fulfillment in the kingdom of God is much more than merely one of the possible interpretations of history—granted that even this one has become impossible for modern man. It represents for the thinking believer the *only* interpretation of history which in his understanding is valid as the expression of man's self-understanding.

Creation means the understanding of space and time as the opportunity for the actualization of that personhood to which we are summoned.

Sin is that act by which we pervert our responsible personhood into its contrary, and by which we become guilty not only in respect to our destiny but also to our environment.

Redemption we experience when we become aware of our perversion and when opportunities present themselves for expiating guilt and righting wrong.

The kingdom of God occurs wherever man knows himself to be absolutely responsible for another in personal community and wherever he attempts to form his world from this attachment.

The Logos of this history—i.e., the special possibility for meaning as the place of the actualization of responsible personhood in community—is Christ as he has been known to believers of all ages as an expression of their self-understanding.

Thinking faith is not limited to this terminology of the Christian faith. It may recognize and actualize its truth without such terminology. But it has no reason to avoid using such terminology if it sees itself in a position to preserve the Christian tradition from distortions, and to express its truth in such a way that it finds in the Christian tradition the appropriate expression for that truth, this discovery only becoming evident through thinking faith's own understanding of the truth of human existence. This last point corresponds to the old principle of the essentially Christian character of the human soul. To bring this truth into being, several things have to be reformed—both with respect to thinking and to the Christian faith. But this is precisely the promising task of a thinking faith.